INSPIRE
YOUR

100 IDEAS
TO RAISE THE BAR

Mark De-Lisser & Dominic Peckham

Illustrations by Ross Crawford

Published 2015 by A&C Black Publishers
an imprint of Bloomsbury Publishing Plc
50 Bedford Square, London, WC1B 3DP

www.bloomsbury.com

Bloomsbury is a registered trademark of Bloomsbury Publishing Plc

978-1-4729-2740-8

Text copyright © Mark De-Lisser and Dominic Peckham
Illustrations © Ross Crawford

Typeset by Newgen Knowledge Works (P) Ltd., Chennai, India
Printed and bound by CPI Group (UK) Ltd, Croydon, CR0 4YY

This book is produced using paper that is made from
wood grown in managed, sustainable forests. It is natural,
renewable and recyclable. The logging and manufacturing
processes conform to the environmental regulations
of the country of origin.

To view more of our titles please visit
www.bloomsbury.com/music

Contents

About the authors

Mark De-Lisser is a vocal coach on BBC's 'The Voice' and lead mentor on Gareth Malone's TV show, 'The Naked Choir'. Driven by his love for teaching, Mark has taught at Westminster University, The BRIT School and The Academy of Contemporary Music, as well as running multiple masterclasses for Kingston University and The British Voice Association. In 2003, Mark formed Singology, a community gospel choir based in central London that has since grown its membership base to include ten additional choirs across the capital. Mark founded the first Gospel Choir at the Academy of Contemporary Music in Guildford. The ACM Gospel Choir went on to become semi-finalists in the BBC's 'Last Choir Standing' in 2008, win the Urban Music Awards for Best Gospel Act 2014, are world record holders for the highest ever carol concert on a plane and have released three studio albums to date.
@markdelisser / www.markdelisser.com

Dominic Peckham is lead mentor on BBC Two's 'The Naked Choir' with Gareth Malone, has served as Vocal Director for the BBC 'Choir of the Year' and is Patron of Voice Festival UK. He is Musical Director of The London Oriana Choir, Artistic Director of The Royal Opera House's 'RM19' Youth Chorus, Assistant Music Director of The National Youth Choirs of Great Britain, Artistic Director and Founder of iSingUK, Artistic Director of The Fourth Choir, Artistic Director of The Ulster Youth Choir, Visiting Lecturer at the University of Oxford and Guest Conductor for Aldeburgh Music, Trinity Laban College of Music and Dance and The London Mozart Players. He regarded as one of the UK's most dynamic young choral conductors and is a passionate ambassador for choral music, through both performance and his educational work across the world.
@dominicpeckham / www.dominicpeckham.com

Introduction

Anyone can start a choir, but we all need some tips and ideas to help us along the way. Here we bring together some of the things we've learned in our experience as choral directors, along with new ideas to keep your choir fresh.

By sharing these lessons from our personal journeys we hope to help you start a choir from scratch, build on established choirs, develop your own musicianship, rehearse effectively, and excel in performance. The 100 practical ideas will give you the toolkit to get through the ruts, provide fresh approaches to old problems and, we hope, enable you to make fantastic music along the way.

The fact that you are reading this book tells us you're on the right track, wanting to be the best you can be and to help your singers create amazing music. Keep going – it's all within grasp!

Mark & Dominic

Acknowledgements

My heartfelt thanks to Mark for this collaboration (and for being generally awesome), Tom for believing in me, my Mum and Dad for opening my young eyes to choirs, and my family and friends for never doubting me. Rachel and Milly for their patience and dedication, Jess and Hannah at Ikon for their unending hard-work, the NYCGB team and all our talented members, Ulster Youth Choir, The London Oriana Choir, The Fourth Choir and to the choral family across the world.

Dominic Peckham

All praise and thanks to God for the amazing opportunities given to me and the ability to make them work and for blessing me with Tracey who has put up with me for all these years. You are my everything! To my kids, Isabella, Isaac and Elias; I couldn't have done this without you all. Your laughter and joy is the best way to end any day when under pressure. To all my choirs and members that I have been in contact with, especially the ACM Gospel Choir and the Singology family. This book exists because of you and how you've inspired me to be better. Lastly, and by no means least, the incredible Dom Peckham for his wonderfulness.

Mark De-Lisser

How to use this book

This book includes ideas for you to dip in and out of in order to improve your choir leading with quick, easy and original ideas.

Each idea includes a summary of the main idea which will catch your eye as you flick through, as well as a step by step guide to implementing the idea.

Each idea also includes one or more of the following:

Top Tip
Practical tips and advice for how to put the idea into practice.

Taking it further...
Ideas and advice for how to extend the idea, develop it further, or make it more challenging.

Involving everyone
Ways to approach the problem involving more people from within your group.

Bonus idea
Ideas that are exciting, extra original and extra interesting.

Anecdotes
Short stories from personal experience.

Part 1
From the top

Starting a choir

"I'm not really sure how it all began. We just got together and had some fun..."

Put simply, you want to sing. And why not, it's one of the greatest and most enjoyable things on this planet and it doesn't cost a penny. It communicates, connects and unites in a unique way. So, if you agree, let's get started!

Start small and start simple – organise a one-off singing experience. Think of your first meeting as an experiment or a bit of fun – keep it relaxed.

Taking it further...

Once there is a buzz about the inevitable success of your first taster, chat to the people who attended and ask them for feedback, comments, or to complete a short survey about how it went (SurveyMonkey.com might be useful). Take those comments on board to make the choir great for everyone.

● Find a venue that isn't too imposing, at minimal cost (ideally free) and has space to stay and socialise afterwards.

● Choose a piece to work on. Be prepared for it to fly or flop, so pick something with this in mind, making sure it is approachable and/or flexible and could work with minimal singers. Ensure you have enough copies of music and a backing track or pianist as necessary.

● Invite friends and as many interested people as you can find to join you for this informal gathering.

● Meet and sing. Even if lots of people cancel and there are only five of you, you must see it through. When those who cancelled hear about it they will just be jealous!

● Keep it short, lasting for one hour maximum. You want people to leave wanting more and having had fun.

Take a photo of the first rehearsal. This will not only be great in your archive as something to look back on, but you can use it as a promotional tool straight away. Get it out there on social media, perhaps with a hashtag #newbeginnings and ask everyone who came and sang to share it with their friends.

Then it's over to you. Write a short action plan with the first steps you need to take clearly laid out. Develop your idea further and refine it based upon the taster session: think about your choir name, the type of music you would like to sing and maybe a logo. Create a short presentation of your ideas and show it to interested individuals and their friends, playing them examples of repertoire the choir might sing. Present it somewhere really relaxed and give them a good flavour of what the choir will be like. Share the excitement and get some core members on board.

Agree some dates for a few first rehearsals and put them in people's diaries. Don't book a concert at first, just get together for fun and keep the rehearsals short. Before you know it, you'll be up and running and wanting to find opportunities to perform.

Involving everyone

Make sure the rehearsal time, venue and day don't exclude people. Picking a time without considering your singers' needs can quickly kill a great idea.

The search begins

"I am about to start a choir – but where do I get members from?"

Sourcing members for a new choir isn't so hard as you might think and neither should it be a great expense.

If you are working with a community choir, then trying to attract members from the local community is always a good idea before going further afield. Finding members for a professional choir will take more administration as they will need to be auditioned to get the right ability and voice-type – you will probably have to look outside your area.

Involving everyone

If you have an existing membership, they can do some of the recruitment for you, engaging their friends and family members and scouting out any potential members to bring along to a taster session.

● Get excited and tell people about your group. Word-of-mouth is powerful, especially if the people you tell can see how excited you are about the choir – they will pass this energy on to any potential members.

● If you have a website, create a sign-up form and collect potential member details that way.

● Use adverts in local newspapers, magazines, fliers, supermarket noticeboards, choir websites and social media (Facebook, Twitter, Meetup, Instagram).

● In any advert, inform people of the rehearsal dates and times for a set period, what type of music you will cover, the level of ability required and any recent performances or future plans.

● Hold an open rehearsal. If you have an existing choir then you can organise a taster session for new members and enable them to join for one rehearsal only and see what it's like. You must be ready to sign up any potential members at these sessions, so be ready – you don't want to miss out on the possible talent.

● If you are holding auditions, choose an accessible venue, choose whether this is a group audition or individual sessions (if the latter, allocate people time slots). You may want to consider whether you want to ask singers to learn something specific in advance, and don't forget to prepare any aural tests you want them to do. It is helpful to have an extra person at auditions to welcome singers as they arrive and ensure auditions in progress are not interrupted. Take photos and make notes in case you need to evaluate people later (memory can fail you) and record the session to further aid your memory. Consider whether you need an accompanist, piano or any other equipment and book an appropriate space accordingly.

● Be prepared. Once you have attracted your singers, you will need to deliver and live up to all you have offered. Make sure the choir and its plans are not just hype and that you have all the material ready for the first sessions and beyond.

Taking it further...

If, when you are spreading the word about your group, you come across instrumentalists, take note of their details in case you need players for a particular event.

Top tip

Some voice parts (tenors, yes) are often harder to recruit than others. Concentrate a little more of your attention on finding these singers and be prepared to continue recruiting throughout the life of your choir.

Finding a good rehearsal space

"Home is where the heart is."

Finding the perfect rehearsal space for your choir will keep your members happy for years to come. It needs to feel like home, but not be so comfortable that they lose focus.

At the very least, your venue should be large, warm, dry and clean enough for your amazing choir but you also need to consider the following:

Taking it further...

Don't go for the cheap option without thinking it through fully. You will be spending a lot of happy times here, so make sure it's comfortable, practical and can grow with you.

❍ Longevity – how long do you want to run your choir for? Assuming that you want your choir to be committed for the long term, your venue should remain constant if possible. Changing it a year or two down the line can have a negative effect on your membership, as people get into routines that become hard to break. Make sure you choose somewhere that can accommodate you for the foreseeable future so that your choir can grow, develop in it and call it home.

❍ Space and light – make sure the venue has enough space so your members can move around and enough light so they can see. Anything too cramped will become uncomfortable. Check out the ventilation and heating in the space; will it get unbearably hot in the summer or really cold in the winter?

❍ Chairs – ensure that you have enough chairs for everybody plus more for any new members as your choir grows.

❍ Equipment – from pianos to PA, does the venue provide for your needs? You don't want to have to bring lots of equipment to every rehearsal.

● Location – the venue needs to be in the right area for your choir. If it is a community choir then being in the heart of the community is important; it creates a hub for your choir and forms part of the group's identity. For a professional choir this can be anywhere your members will travel to without difficulty.

● Noise – you'll be making a fair bit! You do not want to find that you're getting noise complaints from the neighbours. Make sure that anyone living within earshot of the venue is happy to listen to all the wonderful sounds that you are producing and, ideally, get this in writing.

● Opening times – be sure that you know the opening and closing times of the venue. Will you be given a key or will someone open for you? Are these arrangements practical for your group?

● Transport – research public transport and make sure that it's within walking distance of the nearest bus stop or train station, that trains and buses run at the times you rehearse, and that there is sufficient parking nearby.

● Cost – a free venue is a gem, but hard to find. If you do find one it may well be a broom cupboard with a leaky roof, and it may be better to opt for a more suitable venue with a cost that you can afford.

● Tea and cake – have facilities to serve free hot drinks, biscuits and cake. Try not to make your hard-working choir pay for this privilege.

Bonus idea

If you find a venue that is large enough to host a performance, you are on to a real winner. To be able to host a casual concert whenever you like without having to find an alternative space can be really beneficial. Flexible spaces like this do exist, so have a look around.

One Voice, One Vision: aims and objectives

"I'm not really sure how it all started really and I can't remember who came up with the idea."

Singing together is a great shared activity which binds and unifies in a relaxed way. Add some focus to your pursuits by establishing early on what is important to you.

Establish a mission statement – some shared beliefs and aims from the beginning.

Involving everyone

Ask your singers to acknowledge and agree to the mission statement so that beliefs and aims are clear to every member, new or old.

○ Remember why it feels so good to sing with others by writing down all the positives of being in a choir.

○ Highlight which of these are most important to your group.

○ Note down the things you admire and respect about other choirs and would like to see within your own group.

○ If your choir aims to bring together different people within society, work out which groups exactly, their differences, and filter your first two lists so all will be able to get behind the aims you choose.

○ If your choir is about creating amazing music, with precision and vocal excellence, then go for it! But work out how your group will be different from others.

Bonus idea

Consider sending a questionnaire to your potential audience to ask what they want from concerts.

Filter your discoveries and thoughts into a concise mission statement and use this as a catalyst for everything you do and every decision you make.

How many rehearsals?

"I don't want to over-rehearse, but I don't want to be unprepared. How much is 'just right'?"

Rehearsing is essential for the musical growth of any choir. It allows you to develop a unique sound from the voices you have, create soloists, tackle difficult music, build technical excellence, and create cohesion among the singers. But rehearsing too often or too little can be counterproductive.

People like routine and to get involved in activities outside of their day jobs or studies. Rehearsing weekly is generally a good plan for most amateur choirs. This can be done on a term-time basis, which gives your choir good breaks throughout the year. A rehearsal every other week for the whole year is also a good way to work. The key is to enable members to plan their lives around the choir, and not have rehearsals so far apart that people forget what was covered in the last session. But it is important that you allow members to have periods of rest where they have the freedom to do other things. You must also allow breaks for public or religious holidays. Some choirs with more confident singers rehearse based on performances – for the six-to-eight weeks before a concert (or however long is needed to cover the ground).

A two-hour rehearsal is plenty for most people without boredom kicking in. You may want a longer rehearsal close to a major performance but make sure this is announced well in advance so that the members can accommodate it.

Top tip

People are busy so have a strict rehearsal slot and start and finish on time. Even if there are only two people in the room, start on time.

Money, money, money

"I'm not sure whether I should charge my singers or not."

Don't shy away from talking about money. Whether subscription fees, performance fees or expenses, you will have to get involved with money at some point so tackle it and be realistic. All groups have associated costs, whether it's venue hire or your singers' expensive taste in cakes and biscuits, so create an income to keep the choir going and growing.

If you are charging subscription fees, be very clear what you are charging your choir members and when they have to pay it. They should also be aware of the repercussions should they not pay, and the effect that would have on the choir.

Taking it further...

Get organised. Ensure you have a choir bank account and keep things separate from your personal income. You will also need an invoicing system to send invoices out to event organisers to get paid.

○ Be clear about what your overheads are. These will include phone calls, rent for rehearsal space, travel, insurance, music purchases, accompanists and the choir leader's time both in preparation and in front of the choir.

○ Charge a fee that will reasonably cover your expenses with the minimum amount of members that you have – so don't calculate on the basis of 40 singers if you know it may drop off to 20 regulars in future months.

○ See if a monthly or yearly subscription model works best for your choir, and make this known to your members.

○ Sign your members up to direct debits which go straight to the choir bank account.

○ Pay yourself first before your bills. The choir will not run without you so it needs you to be paid to ensure your continued commitment.

If your choir is charging performance fees then be equally clear about what you need to charge for your services. There is a difference between a community choir fee and a professional choir fee. As a rule of thumb, any choir with more full-time singers than amateur is generally considered a professional choir; the majority earn their living from singing. This is not a hard-and-fast rule but you need to be able to fulfil the expectations that will follow. For example, professional choirs will be asked to record an advert at 11am on Tuesday morning. Could your choir fulfil this type of request on a regular basis?

When deciding your fees, be clear about whether you pay your members or whether the money goes into the choir 'pot', and consider:

- How long the choir will need to sing for

- How many singers are needed

- How long people will need to be at the venue

- How far the choir will need to travel

- How singers will travel, and what this will cost

- Your overheads

Organisations such as the Musicians' Union and the Incorporated Society of Musicians can provide advice on fees and hourly rates that your group and singers should be receiving, so do seek specialist advice.

What voice am I?

"One of my biggest worries is starting with singers who don't know what section they should be in, or what voice type they are."

Don't create unnecessary barriers by worrying too much about sections and voice types at the very start. Just get everyone singing, that's all that matters.

Address the problem head-on: 'I know a lot of you don't know what voice you are, or maybe have never sung in parts, but I don't care, I just want to hear you. Let's just have fun singing with one big voice!'

Top tip

Don't be afraid to use the simplest music in concerts, this is quite often the most effective.

○ Start with simple repertoire that can be sung altogether in unison. This way you are building singers' confidence and getting a chance to hear your singers working as one.

○ It's very easy to make a single-voiced piece sound impressive by splitting things up and being creative. Think about solos, body percussion, different tempos and call and response to make your piece sound varied in other ways.

○ Singing in rounds and canon sounds impressive and is a great way to build texture and vocal parts without labelling voice parts too early. These improve listening skills, rhythmic security and intonation between each singer. Try using long phrases to minimise repetition and lengthen the duration of the piece; multiple groups, and changing the number of groups between repetitions; clapping parts or rapping rounds; single-note drones or rhythmic ostinatos to add texture; versions of the phrase with all note values doubled or halved.

By the end of this, you'll have created some great music and have a feel for the vocal ranges of your singers, without it having become an obstacle to getting started.

One size fits all?

"I'm in two different choirs and I like the contrast in sizes between them. I have no favourite; I love them both equally!"

If you're starting from the very beginning with your choir, don't get hung up on how many people you want. Just getting them there is achievement enough.

If you have an established choir and are worried about numbers, just stop and think whether or not it *really* matters – there are no rules about sizes of choirs! Consider the following when deciding what is the right size for you:

● Small chamber choirs work wonderfully but there are real challenges when working with a smaller group – your singers need to be confident on their lines as they have fewer colleagues in their section to support them.

● What repertoire do you want to sing? Some music suits choirs of certain sizes. If you're singing early classical music or popular a cappella, you will probably want a smaller group of singers. If you want to sing barbershop or Verdi, a huge group will work well.

● Listen to how the same piece sounds when sung by both large and small groups. Decide which sounds you like, and which pieces you like that sound applied to – it may well vary across repertoire.

● What about your own confidence and skills? If you only feel comfortable working with choirs of a certain size, consider some training for yourself to learn how to cope with different types of groups.

Taking it further...

If you want to grow your choir, set out a plan and have a target number per voice part. Give yourself a good amount of time to achieve this, perhaps expanding in time for a particular project, anniversary or challenging piece.

Idea 9

A choir with a difference

"How do I make my choir different, special, unique?"

There are thousands of choirs all doing their own thing but they're really not all that different from each other. You can create a choir with a difference, an identity, something special to stand out from the crowd.

Consider the following when putting your choir together or proposing a freshening up of your existing choir.

○ Music and musical arrangement style (classical, early music, pop, rock, vintage, a cappella).

○ Performance style (dance, movement, energetic, avant-garde, statuesque, robotic).

○ Dress style (colours, themes, eras, costume, casual).

○ The voices that make your choir (male, female, children, teens, mixed).

○ Does the choir have a conductor in the traditional sense or is the conductor part of the choir for a more ensemble-style performance, with all focus on the singers?

○ Audience participation.

○ Be creative! The choir is yours, so be imaginative and make it express your uniqueness.

Don't be afraid to try something out and see it fail – knowing what doesn't work for you is often equally helpful.

Bonus idea

Involve your audience. You could ask them to bring blindfolds to have a musically immersive experience without seeing, just hearing.

Anecdote

Recently, I saw a burlesque choir who started their performance in choir robes (you can imagine where it went next). They were also very clever with the lighting. Think outside the box!

Mark

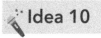

What's your style?

"We're not really sure what to class ourselves as – we just sing!"

Instrumental groups would need to change personnel and instruments in order to diversify the styles of music they can perform. Singers don't, so count yourself lucky and enjoy the versatility of your group.

If you want to focus on a particular style of music, that's fine – but don't create unnecessary parameters which close possibilities that would be good for you. As you discover how you sound together and evolve with time you may want to try different repertoire. You have a great flexibility with voices – use this to your advantage.

To get ideas of genre which will suit you:

● Make a note of your 20 favourite choral pieces and other songs that you would like to perform with this group. See where they fit in the broader musical landscape and let them form the basis of the style you work in. They will spark complementary repertoire choices.

● Think about what type of music suits a choir of your size. Listen to other similar groups, and the repertoire they sing, and how you think it sounds.

● Look at websites about choral music and find lists of group classifications and genres. Choral associations may help, for example the American Choral Directors Association (ACDA) website (acda.org).

● Explore how these different groups sound.

● Set yourself a timetable of genres to try. Consider which will be easier and which will be more challenging, and approach them in an appropriate order. Evaluate what feels right for your group.

> **Top tip**
>
> You don't need to label yourself to attract people to your music: simply list both the composers and songs or pieces in your promotion and then it's really clear.

Icebreaker

"I want to get the singers involved in the session quickly. What can I do to make them lose their inhibitions?"

By communicating with each other using their singing voices, singers will loosen up and be ready to make music on into the night. Keep this idea fun and allow people to laugh and be themselves.

In this activity singers create a great soundscape at the start of a rehearsal. This allows singers to connect with each other and relax into making music together in a fun and energising way. Each singer starts with the collective strength of his or her group and then, by asking the singers to move around, you are creating an easy progression for them towards solo work, without losing the group support. Here are step-by-step instructions for how to put the idea into action.

Top tip

Make sure you, the leader, also get involved and move around, communicating with passing singers using a motif. Be playful and free and you will create a great working atmosphere.

● Split the choir into three mixed groups (not voice parts).

● Set a pulse that the choir can click along to.

● Give each group a melody line, a percussive part or vocal sound that they all sing together. Each part should fit together with the others to create a short (two-to-four-bar) a cappella motif.

● Once all the parts are secure and working together, ask the singers to walk freely through the space, keeping the pulse and continuously singing their part as they move around.

● While walking, as they pass those on different parts, they must greet singers using their own line to communicate with that person. They should try and convey a 'Hi, how are you' with their vocal part.

● End the exercise by bringing everyone back to standing still wherever they are, and then end the singing.

Local events such as fun days, community events, fundraising events and religious festivals are also great opportunities to perform. If the event is outdoors, remember to think about amplification (see Idea 64) or you may not be heard.

Part 2
Preparation and organisation

A failsafe rehearsal plan

"How much material do I need in a rehearsal?"

Make sure that you have a good robust plan for each session so that you cover everything, keep interest and are not left floundering in front of your choir.

Pick a focus for all of the rehearsal (all pieces and warm-ups). This may be dynamics, blend or communication. Then follow this rehearsal plan, and you won't go far wrong:

Taking it further...

Send each section into a different room so they can rehearse their part in isolation. You will need a section leader who knows their part well enough to guide the group. Reassemble the choir towards the end of the session to put the parts back together.

○ Warm up. Choose warm-ups that prepare your singers physically, mentally and vocally so that they are ready to tackle the challenges of your repertoire.

○ Start the warm-ups as soon as the rehearsal begins – get singing straight away.

○ Say what you would like to achieve during the rehearsal.

○ Have something prepared to use if the rehearsal progresses quicker than expected or if something planned doesn't work very well.

○ At the end of the session, have one last sing-through of all the pieces. Articulate a specific goal for this final run-through and don't just 'sing it again'.

○ Warm down and announce any new information that the members need to know for the next session (keep this short – a couple of minutes only).

○ Answer any questions from the singers.

○ Finish the session on time – respect your singers' time, and they will respect yours.

Warm-ups – why bother?

"Warm-ups waste my rehearsal time and are boring and repetitive, I really don't see the point."

Warm-ups are crucial when developing any choir and can determine the success of your rehearsals. They bring focus to the learning atmosphere within the room, reset busy minds and prepare your singers physically. Warm-ups are also the first collective output from your group in each session and therefore act as a team-building exercise.

● Kick off with instant call and response sequences, such as clapping rhythms, or physical movement. This grabs attention and silences the room without you having to say a word.

● Work in a circle.

● Bring your singers into the action by asking for one-on-one responses where appropriate.

● Make your warm-ups work for you by integrating some of your specific learning objectives for that session.

● Create your own physical and vocal exercises so your choir becomes familiar with them and their outcomes, but update and add to these through the year to keep them fresh and relevant.

● Explain clearly what you're doing, and why. If your singers understand the benefits of warming up, then they will respect the process more.

● Remind each section (or individuals) of challenges from the previous rehearsal and connect the technical aspects of your warm-ups to those challenges.

● Congratulate or encourage individuals where appropriate.

● Ask questions – "Can someone remind me why we're doing this?"

Top tip

Avoid scales – singers don't benefit from clunky vertical movement of scales like instrumentalists do and they don't need to develop their muscle memory in the same way. Work with glissandi 'sirens' instead.

Taking it further...

Ask choir members to lead parts of the warm-up. This inclusivity can also serve as an assessment tool to see what they understand about the exercises.

Sorry I'm late, again...

"My members are always late and it frustrates me and cuts down our rehearsal time."

Punctuality is crucial in any choir, new or old. If you allow people to be constantly late, your members will think it is acceptable and this attitude will become hard to reverse.

Involving everyone

There may be some members who are not able to arrive on time. Does this cause a major problem? If it does, explore starting at an alternative time. Make sure you do this based on singers' feedback, as you don't want to make things difficult for a different group of people.

Creating good habits of punctuality will make your choir strong. A key point to understand is that your singers will adopt the discipline that you display, so this all begins with you, whatever you do will be taken by your choir members to be usual practice. Remember, finishing on time is also good punctuality as this sets up boundaries that members can structure their lives around – they are more likely to respect a start time if you respect an end time!

The way you conduct your rehearsals in terms of punctuality is also how your choir will behave when turning up for the all-important concert performances. If you can get your choir into the right habits at the very beginning, it will be much easier later on.

◉ Arrive early.

◉ Ensure all equipment is set up before the start time of the rehearsal.

◉ Start the rehearsal on time with whomever you have in the room at that point.

◉ Finish on time.

This is a simple problem and therefore the actions are simple. You will be amazed at how quickly people fall into good practice.

Achievable targets

"It's suddenly all a little bit bewildering and I can't believe the concert is so soon!"

Stay realistic with your concerts and programming and don't overwhelm your choir.

First and foremost, work out what you want to achieve for your forthcoming project or in your concert.

● Decide on the length of performance, keeping in mind audience attention-span and the stamina of your singers.

● Think carefully about repertoire. Don't be afraid to programme lots of small pieces rather than one huge piece. It's much easier to prepare small chunks.

● Consider giving the concert variety by using different singers for different pieces. This also gives your singers rests.

● Once you have an idea of the repertoire, look at how many rehearsals you have and place the pieces within these. You may need to delete items or adjust your programme.

● Expect to need to cover a piece four times extensively before expecting everyone to be 'gig ready'.

● Ensure that your singers know in advance what they are rehearsing from week to week so that they can come prepared.

● Sometimes we are all guilty of a stop-start rehearsal, fixing tiny details. This can tire your singers quickly, and in many cases running things from start to finish a few times results in things 'coming out in the wash'!

Involving everyone

Why don't you ask your more advanced singers or section leaders to let you know of problem areas? They could compile their own checklist and note what they feel they need more time on.

Getting your choir to focus

"My choir love being together, but so much that they lose concentration."

All choir members must be focused if they are to make any progress. They will all get so much more from the experience if they bring their full attention to the session each week and give it their all.

Involving everyone

Appoint someone within each section to monitor where people sit and make sure it varies from week to week.

◉ Remove any back-row mentality by moving your singers around each week.

◉ Start work on a piece by playing your singers a good recording. Encourage them to absorb the atmosphere and digest the sound. Time is often limited, so giving the singers the chance to understand the piece in its entirety and have a listen with copies of the music in front of them could make a huge difference.

◉ Clearly set out what you expect from each rehearsal by publishing a full schedule of what you will work on each week and exactly what you want to achieve in each session. Circulate it in advance so your singers can come prepared, knowing what is ahead of them.

◉ Remind the group each week how many sessions are left before the next performance.

◉ Create a playlist of the pieces that you are working on and share this with your singers, asking them to listen to them three times before the rehearsal.

◉ Remind your choir that rehearsals don't stay still. They move forward, and each session should feel like a step up as you get closer to your event.

● Always start the next section of rehearsals by reviewing any previous work done on this music and the pitfalls and challenges already identified. Otherwise you may find yourself correcting the same mistakes each week.

● When you make a comment, allow the choir some time to digest what you have said. It's very easy to correct a problem, or point out issues and then move on too quickly. Ask them what they think they can do to improve and what they might need to note on their scores or lyric sheets to make sure that can happen.

● Record or film your rehearsal: getting a positive focus to the session comes out of a shared understanding of what you're trying to achieve, so reviewing your work on film or audio will help every individual see the group's potential for improvement and development more clearly.

⭐ **Bonus idea**

Develop a listening rota. Each week, ask one person to sit behind you to listen and absorb the full sound of the rehearsal rather than singing. Don't forget that choir members rarely hear the full sound or experience what you hear because they're too busy singing. So, by having another set of ears you are not only sharing responsibility and getting opinions from choir members but allowing them to hear all parts equally.

Shut up and listen!

"I find it so hard to get the other singers to be quiet when I'm teaching a different part. Help me!"

Teaching a number of different voice parts in a rehearsal session can be difficult, as there will be times when some singers are waiting and have nothing to do. Here's a simple way to approach rehearsals, which helps tackle this problem and also adds new learning dimensions to the practice time.

Bonus idea ⭐

Teach the whole choir all parts where range permits and develop your singers' understanding of the piece.

When learning a song for the first time, start by teaching a good chunk of the melody to all the voice parts at the same time – even if it's not their part. In a song with a simple structure, the verse and chorus should work well, or in a classical piece choose a small section of the piece (this doesn't have to be the opening). When this has been learned by everybody, teach a single additional part, while the other sections continue to sing the first melody altogether. Continue this process until all the parts have been learnt for that section. Repeat the same approach for any additional sections of the song.

Taking it further...

This is a particularly good exercise for times when you are short of people in a section. If everyone has learned the melody it can be easy to swap around between voice parts to balance the sound.

By teaching music in this way you expose the singers' ears to the main melody first. They can then easily understand where their part fits within the harmony and in relation to the melody. This will help them understand the shape and structure of the arrangement, the relative importance of the individual lines, and should be beneficial for their intonation. Some singers may struggle initially to hold two parts in their head but over time this will become a valuable skill.

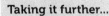

What are the lyrics again?

"Some of my members just can't remember their words. It can be such a pain."

Getting people to learn lyrics off by heart will mean that they can focus more on emotion and delivery, plus they will be looking more in your direction for the cues. For some people, however, singing from memory can be tricky.

Stimulating all the senses at once while listening to the music is a really good way of learning lyrics. Here is a strategy for using different senses to aid memory.

For this, you will need printed copies of the lyrics or music for each singer, pens, paper and a recording of the piece. Then, read through the four ideas below and give them a go:

1. Aural learning: Play the piece all the way through in order to get an understanding of the structure. Then, play it again pausing after every line or phrase.

2. Kinaesthetic learning: During the first play of the piece, ask the singers to note down the structure as they hear it. On the second time through during the pauses, the singers should write out the words, adding any drawings that enhance the meaning of the phrases.

3. Oral learning: While writing each word, the singers should say or sing the phrase.

4. Visual learning: During the exercise, singers should always be looking at the printed words, their handwritten versions and their drawings.

Taking it further...

This exercise can be done outside of rehearsal too. Encourage your choir members to do this when practising at home.

Top tip

Typing the word on a tablet or phone doesn't have the same result. The singers can listen on their phones and tablets so that they can control the length of the pauses themselves, but make sure pens and paper are used for step two.

Listen and learn

"Not many of my members read music. What can I do?"

Teaching by ear can be a challenge for those who have developed the skill of reading music but it doesn't have to be daunting and can be a very good skill to develop. It does require a little more preparation, but the results can be quite amazing.

Whether or not you prefer to use sheet music, be prepared for your singers to need to hear their part to learn it. You can do this for music you have arranged by ear, a notated arrangement, or pop or classical pieces – it doesn't matter.

Taking it further...

Research resources which provide demonstration parts for singers along with scores (e.g. Mark's Sing Out! series) or just demonstrations (www.choircake.com).

● Know every part of the song well yourself. This is essential to teaching by ear.

● Divide the song into manageable chunks and within these small sections teach each voice part their line before moving on.

● Use the 'call and response' technique, where you sing a line and the singers repeat it back to you. If you lack confidence in demonstrating, practise singing through the parts before you arrive at your rehearsal.

● Ask the singers to repeat each part over and over until secure.

● Record the parts as audio (over a backing track or click) and play these as required when teaching. This way you don't have to keep the parts in your head and the recording will always be right – assuming you've recorded them correctly, of course. Some publications provide isolated parts along with the music – this might be useful for you.

● Allow your singers to take the recordings home or let them know where to get them.

Change it up

"I want to make sure that no one is ever bored in my rehearsals."

The way you view your rehearsals, and how you stage them can aid learning, so change it up and get your choir out of rows!

Different positions will work for different pieces, and when working on different aspects of the music. Think about which other parts people need to hear most clearly to achieve the best results. Here are some ideas to get you started.

○ Traditional arrangements can be varied, for example in blocks ordered from high to low (SATB), having sopranos and altos on a front row with tenors and basses behind, putting the lower parts in the middle (STBA or SABT).

○ Practise in circles so that your singers can hear as much as possible.

○ Create 'mini choirs' with a well-balanced part representation in each and send them off to work in small groups. It will increase individual confidence and less confident singers will be strengthened.

○ Scatter all voice parts around the space.

○ Ask the singers to turn their back to you – they will have to listen very carefully!

○ Scramble (see Idea 21)

○ Ask your singers to do a physical movement when they have the tune, e.g. stand up or raise a hand in the air.

○ Could you rehearse in your concert venue? The extra time spent rehearsing in an unfamiliar space is very valuable. It may cost, but it may be worth it.

Top tip

Don't be afraid to stop conducting and walk to the back of your venue to see how the music will sound to an audience, how the music and words carry through the space, and how the singers cope without you.

Scrambling

"My singers are getting a bit lazy in rehearsals. How can I keep them 'on it'?"

If your singers are in a daydream during a rehearsal, looking at phones, tweeting, 'liking' a photo or checking the football score, keep the session challenging by mixing things up a little. Here we try moving our singers so that they are physically further away from other members of their section.

Taking it further...

To increase the challenge, do this with material as it is being learned for the first time.

Bonus idea

Once you have tried this a few times and if you have the space to move around, ask your choir to walk around the room while singing. This way the sound around them is constantly changing which in turn creates new challenges.

○ Prepare a list of songs or pieces the choir are already familiar with.

○ Start your rehearsal as normal, but with each member beside someone from another section. Each singer should have a singer from a different section on either side.

○ Sing through one of the pieces and ask the members how they found the experience. What did they have to focus on more? What did they find difficult? Did it positively influence anything?

○ The sound will be different, so feed back to the choir on how the sound changed, what suffered and what improved.

○ Try the next piece in new positions, but still scrambled, perhaps spreading out even more within the space, so the singers are more aware of their own voices.

○ End the exercise with a break for tea and cake!

○ Use this exercise regularly. It will not only help the singers to increase their concentration levels, but also consolidate their knowledge of their part.

The Pressure Cooker

"How do I make sure all the singers are completely confident with their parts?"

When choirs are large in membership it can be difficult to gauge who knows their parts and who might be struggling. The Pressure Cooker idea will give you the information you need and will help develop the ability of your singers at the same time.

In any choir, some people will have stronger voices than others. Don't overlook the singers who are earlier on in their journey: knowing that they are secure with their part is key to improving the overall quality of the choir's sound. This idea will put the singers under some pressure but you can adapt it to make it less of a struggle for your developing singers.

Once you have taught your group a new piece, try the following:

1. Ask for volunteers from each section. Select between one and three singers for each voice part – having three per part will make it a less daunting task for developing singers.

2. Ask the volunteers to stand at the front of the room and perform the piece from start to finish as best as they can.

3. Rotate the singers until everyone within the choir has been in the spotlight.

4. If you don't have an even number of singers across the sections, ask stronger singers to stand in a number of times.

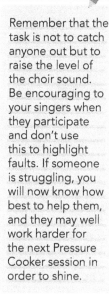

Top tip

Remember that the task is not to catch anyone out but to raise the level of the choir sound. Be encouraging to your singers when they participate and don't use this to highlight faults. If someone is struggling, you will now know how best to help them, and they may well work harder for the next Pressure Cooker session in order to shine.

Creative improvisation

"I've tried to encourage my choir to improvise but they're very reluctant to try."

Improvisation can be a daunting experience but it can also be liberating and fun. Here we look at how we can involve everyone to build confidence in their creativity.

• Stand in a circle formation.

• Set the pulse with a two-finger clap (audible but not overpowering) – all the choir claps along to the beat.

• Step into the middle of the circle and sing a short melody, then ask the choir to repeat it back.

• Repeat, creating four melodies that the choir repeat as a call and response.

• Once you have completed your four melodies, take it in turns so that each member has a turn at standing in the circle and creating their own four melodies. (If some singers feel that they can't create a melody as easily as others they should be encouraged to take inspiration from other members or just sing something very simple such as a sustained note.) As in your initial demonstration, the choir immediately sings back each melody after it is sung, keeping to the same beat.

• You can end the exercise when everyone has contributed. Encouraging all singers to take part in this activity, and not just volunteers, will help them to enjoy their own voices and become more confident in creating melodies.

You are your brother's keeper

"Teamwork makes the dream work."

Singers in choirs sometimes think that they stand alone in their sections and believe that if they are the best and know their part better than the person next to them, they are doing really well. This is one of the most counterproductive thoughts that your singers can have and it is your responsibility to change that mindset.

A collective identity should be encouraged within voice parts. This may bring some friendly competition between sections but not individual singers.

● Encourage your singers in every rehearsal to work collaboratively to learn the parts.

● Remind them that they are working with their colleagues to create a blended single voice – there are no prizes for hearing single voices in a choir.

● Encourage the choir to listen to the other singers in their section and help where needed.

● Ask them to highlight mistakes only when this is a repeated error and not just a slip, and only when they can help them to resolve the issue.

● Encourage everyone to receive help offered by their colleagues gladly and objectively.

● If the issue cannot be resolved or there is a difference of opinion, they should consult you as the leader for clarification.

Taking it further...

Have a 'sing-off' where sections perform a part of a song that they are currently learning to the rest of the group. Set a focus for the challenge and critique, such as blend, dynamics, phrasing, communication or energy. Allow some time for the sections to work on this before they perform, and choose one winner only.

🎤 Part 3
In rehearsal

Play the game

"Sometimes it's just nice to stop all forms of work and play a game."

Games are a great way to focus your room, unite all participants and get everyone working as a team. Whether at the beginning, middle or end of a rehearsal they are such a great moment of downtime, you may find your singers actively look forward to them.

Involving everyone

Consider asking individuals from your choir to come up with (and lead) games themselves in an effort to take the pressure off you, and create a less formal outlook on proceedings.

● Research group games and activities and maybe ask colleagues and friends too (sometimes word of mouth with these things uncovers the best results).

● Develop a repertoire of a few games that you know inside out.

● Try and make sure that the game promotes some of the qualities, attributes and skills that you're looking to develop in your choir such as counting, watching or listening.

Try 'Never Say Nine' – this is perfect for rhythmic accuracy and pulse awareness.

● Standing in a circle, each person is responsible for saying one number in the sequence (one to eight).

● It must be said in time, so start slowly!

● Count your group in, 'five, six, seven, eight' to set the pulse, and then begin.

● The group will start counting, one number per person around the circle. If someone says a number out of time or says the forbidden number nine, the group will together shout, either 'Down you go, you're too slow' or 'Never say nine!' depending on which one is appropriate.

Identity and pride

"We've got a clear identity and big personalities, but no one in our audience seems to see that."

Choirs are all shapes and sizes, so where do you fit in? Work out what makes you great and shout about it.

● Remember your mission statement (see Idea 4). You should be able to distil this and sum up your choir simply within two sentences, maximum.

● If your choir has a clear identity – e.g. a university a cappella group, an LGBT choir, a gospel choir – decide how you are going to portray this. Help the wider world to understand who you are by including a short line which conveys the essence of your group in all promotional material and on your social media profiles.

● Testimonials are very powerful when promoting your identity, so get your members to write a short sentence about what your choir means to them. Put them in your programmes or on your website along with a photo of the choir member.

● Group photos and concert shots are such a good way to show your singers' enthusiasm for your choir, so snap away at rehearsals and gigs and share the news and images from your recent engagements on your websites, blogs and on social media.

● Put pictures of your choir members and a brief bit of information about them on your website. You could keep this light and non-musical, e.g. their favourite film.

● Your members should feel proud of posters, logos and any other imagery your choir uses. Do things properly and allow them to input (or take charge) and come up with materials they want to share.

Taking it further...

Ask your members to write blogs or short articles about the rehearsal process or your last concert. Publish them in concert programmes or on your website.

Positive vibes

"Your choir looks so joyful. I wish my group were a bit happier!"

Creating a positive environment within your choir helps the choir perform better in both rehearsal and performance.

Taking it further...

Delegating certain aspects of managing the choir is a great way of getting everyone involved, but make sure things are shared and no one is overburdened.

○ Engage your members in personal conversation. This is not always possible with large groups but do make your general chat to the choir more human and less business-like. Let them get to know you and your personality – the key to this is honesty. A leader who shows his or her faults as well as strengths builds a stronger bond with the choir.

○ Speak to individuals in breaks, especially those you know less well.

○ Appreciate your choir. Giving the choir a 'pat on the back' shouldn't just be praise for a successfully completed task but also throughout the process.

○ Saying 'thank you' will make the choir feel appreciated and that you have noted their efforts.

○ Always listen to your singers. Sometimes members know best and have good ideas that you will just not have thought of, so assess these ideas and try and enable them to come to life where possible.

○ Listen to musical requests. Whether an arrangement or a repertoire idea, allowing your members to get involved shows that you appreciate and respect them.

○ Trust your members. This can be shown in many ways. You could ask individuals to lead a warm-up or part of the rehearsal, or to select some songs for an upcoming performance.

○ Schedule social activities into your year. There's nothing like good food and company to keep your choir happy.

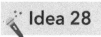

Crack the whip

"My conductor is really fun and approachable, but I wouldn't want to get on the wrong side of him."

Balancing the need to be in control and being friendly can be difficult, but you do need to remain professional and authoritative.

○ Create a professional working environment in rehearsals. Singers need to understand that you are there to do a job and that you are taking that responsibility seriously.

○ Avoid asking your singers to be quiet. Expect quiet, be quiet, and they'll get the message.

○ Wait for quiet before giving instructions – you're giving valuable information which your singers need to hear fully.

○ Create a 'no passengers' rule. Each singer needs to give the same level of focus and commitment.

○ Be ready and prepared. Always be at the front of your choir, ready to start five minutes before you are due.

○ Respect and discipline go hand in hand so make sure you finish your rehearsals and stop for breaks on time.

Top tip
If you're returning to a piece and what you learned last session has been forgotten, let your choir know you're disappointed. It's a two-sided effort, so remind everyone that both you and the singers need to be on top of things.

○ If you need to challenge an individual directly, a friendly public approach may work best initially, before speaking with them on their own.

○ Be direct. Occasionally ask people what they have written down following your instructions. This will make sure they are annotating things and working individually to improve and take on board your comments.

○ Asking individuals to recap what you've been working on is an effective way to get people to take the rehearsal seriously – make people aware that they may be asked a question or to perform at any time.

○ Ask your section leaders to help you maintain a hard-working space.

Hitting a rut, and how to get out of it

"Something's not right. We've got good repertoire, a great team and enough singers, but the rehearsals don't feel like fun for me or them. I think it's all got a bit serious."

Sometimes, through no fault of your own, you'll hit a rut. It might be caused by the music, technical issues, or group dynamics, but it's solvable.

Involving everyone

Try being totally honest and transparent with the choir and schedule a feedback session. Plan some questions in advance to lead the discussion about how the choir works. Your singers will see that you are listening to them. They will know that you're doing your best to get back on track and will be more likely to support you in this journey.

Social development and interaction is as important as the artistic elements of running a choir, if not more important. If there are frictions between people, these will be reflected in the music, or have a negative effect on your rehearsal time. Plan a number of non-singing events to boost morale and strengthen relationships within the choir.

● Have social events and place them carefully. If you can predict when difficult times occur (for example just after a concert or midway through a rehearsal schedule), try putting the social events in these periods to maintain momentum.

● Be creative and think outside the box for ways to reignite the buzz. Would a team-building exercise work for your group? Or a stag or hen-do type of event? You could all go for a dance lesson, have a themed meal night, hold a 'bake-off' challenge or do a team sport together.

● Acknowledging people's birthdays will make them feel valued. Do this, especially if a birthday falls on a rehearsal or concert day. Could you or a singer write and arrange a custom version of *Happy Birthday* and the group learn to sing it?

If your problems are musical or vocal, then you need to change course and approach things differently.

● If you can isolate a particular technical issue, ask your professional colleagues for alternative ways to tackle the problem. Networks are an invaluable creative resource.

● If a particular piece is causing a problem and not progressing, think about finding a way to simplify it or make a change to your programme and abandon it completely.

● Listen to a recording of the pieces you are learning together. Your singers rarely hear and comprehend a piece as a whole. This renewed sense of destination and awareness of the 'end product' may be just what you need.

● Bring in a guest to work with the choir. A guest could work either as part of the existing rehearsals or as a separate workshop day. Singers will experience different aspects of working together and a new set of musical demands. A change is as good as a rest!

Taking it further...

Go to a concert together. Find groups, choirs, artists that you admire and plan a trip to watch them perform live. Hearing music with fellow singers makes such a difference and inspires people to raise their game and aim high.

Bonus idea

You could try having an anonymous suggestion box at all rehearsals, to allow sensitive issues to be brought to your attention confidentially and without friction.

Sectional leaders

"I don't have enough hands, eyes or ears to deal with everything."

Empowering people to serve as section leaders is a good way of developing the musicianship within the ranks of your choir.

Involving everyone

Consider changing sectional leaders each year to give more members this opportunity. This is not essential, but when you see people who are flourishing it is great to acknowledge this by giving them responsibility.

Sectional leaders should be responsible for the other singers sharing their voice part. Any problem, musically or otherwise, can be passed to you, but they can be the first port of call and should aim to make sure that all singers in their section are secure on their part and clear about what they are doing. They become your additional eyes and ears and you can encourage them to fix musical discrepancies as the rehearsal progresses. To do this effectively, they need to know the material well and be confident to demonstrate their part if needed. Don't choose sectional leaders for their vocal ability alone (although this does help), they need to be approachable, caring in nature and confident socially. Don't treat them as any better than others, but as a crucial element within the learning process and a link between you and all individuals. If you have the time and space, try a rehearsal where the section leaders take their colleagues to a separate room to rehearse their part in isolation. This will help them gain more focus and allow them to iron out any issues before returning to sing with the whole choir towards the end of the rehearsal.

Dead wood

"I have some singers that aren't cutting it. What can I do?"

Every choir will have members who are not so strong as others. As a leader you can choose whether to ignore the problems, hope they will leave, or tackle them to make them stronger. Here we consider working to improve their ability.

● Work out what those individuals' strengths are and where these can be used immediately. This will keep them feeling valued.

● Ascertain aspects which need development and work out a strategy for improvement.

● Consider splitting the choir into different abilities to give more focus and time to the developing singers who may be being swamped and intimidated by the stronger singers. This will take more time, as you will probably need a separate rehearsal for them, but it will be worthwhile.

● Encourage the singers who may have specific vocal issues to commit to some individual lessons with a singing teacher or trusted musician you recommend.

● Make sure they are given an easier, more supported part where that is an option.

Be sensitive when telling singers they need improvement. It may not be taken well, so make sure your message is your desire to help them improve and fulfil the potential you see in them.

Anecdote

Once I split my choir due to the differences in ability. Some people left, saying that I didn't value them. This was not the case – I wanted to give them a chance to improve in an environment where they could be heard. The ones who stayed have blossomed into great singers and have gone on to more demanding musical activities and account this to being pushed to improve.

Mark

Considering a cull? Meet it head on!

"I work so hard in this choir, and I think the standard has really improved, but there are one or two people who just don't seem to care about getting better.'

If you're trying to keep improving your choir you are on the right track, but everyone in your choir also needs to be on board. It may be that you have to make the difficult decision of asking someone to leave for the benefit of everyone.

Involving everyone

Managing a problem should involve as much positive action as possible, so make sure you praise where possible and keep in touch with any individuals you are concerned about to show that you are 100% supporting their efforts to improve.

Through personal development and hard work, your rehearsals and your choir's technical ability should be improving. You should see a difference in vocal ability, tone and technique, and begin to try some more exciting and challenging repertoire. But, let's face it, there may be some members who just won't join with you on that journey. It is not necessarily about the standard of singing or musicianship; some people who struggle vocally or musically can have an attitude and determination which is an invaluable positive influence on and inspiration to the group. This makes them as worthy as anyone to be part of the team. Your role is not to try and be Alan Sugar, but sometimes you need to talk frankly with individuals about whether or not they are fully committed.

● The moment you've identified any problems or concerns with individuals it is time to be honest – communicate with them.

● Give them a chance to improve in the areas that are concerning you; allow singers at least two months to turn things around.

● Make sure you speak to them in a way which

reflects the ethos of the group. To talk about how the issue is negatively affecting the team is a good approach and how they react will give you an indication of whether or not change is going to come.

○ Offer support. Can you arrange for some lessons with a singing teacher or a trusted musician? If the problem is with attitude, could you ask another singer to help by mentoring and modelling appropriate behaviour?

○ If support and encouragement is not working, you may need to ask them to find another more suitable group. Invite them to re-audition in the future when they have worked on the particular issues causing problems.

It can be difficult, but significant misdirection could result in a stagnant group, everyone's hard work being wasted and a discouraged, falling membership. The benefits of a cull are clear to see – everyone will be pulling their socks up as they are reminded that this choir only works if they make the difference and put the work in.

Bonus idea

Can you find a local singing teacher and musician to get on board and support your choir? They could hold some surgery sessions for choir members who need some intensive or one-on-one support.

Please don't go!

"I'm worried my singers will leave. I want them to be happy and enjoying themselves."

The membership is the lifeblood of any choir. The singers *are* the choir and without them you are just a soloist! Keeping them happy is key to retaining them and not just sustaining your choir but encouraging its growth.

- Choose repertoire relevant to the choir members. Don't just pick your favourite songs, choose music they will enjoy or will help them to develop.
- Challenge them to broaden their musicality by introducing different types and styles of music.
- Create opportunities for soloists to shine.
- Listen to their feedback: ask them what they like and dislike about the choir. Discuss their needs, ambitions and goals.
- Make sure you are moving the rehearsals at the right speed – too fast or slow will be very frustrating for the singers.
- Ask about your singers' other skills and interests and make use of them where possible.
- Be approachable and always on hand to answer any questions.
- Make them feel like it's their choir too by asking their opinions before making a major decision.
- Create performance opportunities regularly to keep the choir excited and engaged.
- Create a buddy system, where members check up on their buddy if they are not at rehearsal.
- Encourage a family-oriented environment.

Blend vs great solo voices

"Can a soloist be a great choir singer too? What is best to have in my group?"

There are many singers who are fantastic soloists and you probably have some within your choir. It is important though that they work hard to be an excellent choral singer too – they need to be a team player as well as a lead singer. This requires the ability to blend and listen to others.

To have a strong all-round choir you need to have a combination of ensemble singers and soloists.

● Have more choral singers than soloists across your choir. If you have soloists who are able to blend well you are sonically in a good place, but if they have limited time or commitment to give to the choir, this could leave you high and dry.

● Some singers want to be heard above everyone else, and while this is great when singing a solo, singers need to fall back in with the overall choir blend and sound at all other times.

● Key soloists: have five or six key singers who between them can cover a solo of any vocal range. This keeps your repertoire options open.

● A blend of all voices within the choir is key to an excellent sound. Work hard on developing this with the singers.

● Give the soloists time to shine. You may feel that they take all the glory for a brilliant solo, but do let them have their moment.

● Develop new soloists. Singers can grow in ability really quickly if given the time, so develop your less-experienced singers and give them solos in relaxed and less pressured concerts.

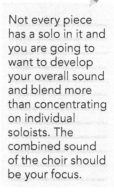

Top tip

Not every piece has a solo in it and you are going to want to develop your overall sound and blend more than concentrating on individual soloists. The combined sound of the choir should be your focus.

Part 4
Developing
your singers

Keeping the beat

"We're getting slower and slower and...what do I do?"

Keeping in time can be surprisingly tricky. Perhaps heads are in the music, the rhythms are tricky, the words are complex, or people just can't 'feel the beat'. Here are some ideas to secure the underlying pulse.

Bonus idea

Play the game 'Never say nine'. (See Idea 25.)

○ Use a metronome throughout the rehearsal, even in the warm-ups. If you are singing a cappella then a steady audible click can help keep everyone on the same page (or beat). Spend the whole rehearsal locking in to the beat.

○ Backing tracks. If you use backing tracks, the hard work in keeping the pulse is done for you. If you don't sing with tracks, using them as a one-off could help embed that feeling of a steady beat in your singers.

○ Make the beat physical and get moving! Give your singers simple movements like a step, click, hand clap, foot stamp, or combination of these, to make the pulse physical.

○ Thigh tap. Progress to a smaller movement that will not detract from the sound while you are rehearsing.

○ The pulse is often lost because singers are stumbling over words, notes or both. If a piece has a danger area, unpick what could be causing this – is it the slow delivery of consonants? Take the passage slower but with an equally firm sense of pulse, using one of the suggestions above, and bring the tempo back up gradually.

Tricky rhythms

"My choir just can't stay in time, they always rush."

With a big group of singers, it's hard to get everyone singing in time with one another, especially when the rhythms get complex. Here are some helpful tips for the times you find your choir speeding up or slurring through challenging sections.

● In the early stages of learning a piece, encourage each singer to tap the pulse somewhere on the body while they sing.

● Start by focusing in on tough rhythmical sections and consolidate these passages while tapping.

● Rap or speak the passages to the correct rhythm.

● Clap the rhythm.

● It is sometimes useful to dance or physically respond to difficult rhythms. It can help your singers internalise the beat.

● Sing the passage staccato, possibly to a 'doo' or a 'ba'. Making everything short and sharp (even the long notes) will highlight where people are not together and bring the focus required to ensure careful rhythmic placement.

● Continue to sing the passage staccato at a very quiet dynamic, but with full support and energy.

● If you find that your choir is going out of time at any point, go back to focusing on small sections using one of the techniques above

Bonus idea

Once or twice a year, consider a session on improving pulse and rhythm. Get in touch with someone who might be willing to come in and run a class for your choir. A local percussionist or a body percussionist will have some great ways to 'feel the rhythm'.

360° musicianship

"Some of my singers tend to rely on others and assume that they don't need to work so hard in a group."

Singing in a choir requires you not just to focus on your own voice but to be very aware of everything that's going on around you – it's a group activity and a team sport!

○ Create a checklist of what your singers should be thinking about when singing. It doesn't need to all happen at once, but building up the listening skills and self-awareness is important.

○ Listening, breathing, dynamics, physical alignment, consonant clarity and vowel sounds all need to be unified, so people need to work hard to listen to their colleagues and create a matched sound in every way.

○ Ask your singers questions about various aspects of the music they're singing, for example, "What dynamic is this?" "Why doesn't this sound right?" "This sounded excellent. What were you doing differently?" This will help them to analyse their own sound as well as the sound of the choir. It also works as a reminder of what you've worked on if you are revisiting previously rehearsed music.

○ Why not write a review of your rehearsals and email your choir members a list of what you've done and what to remember for the next rehearsal? It will help to improve the way they prepare and work in between rehearsals.

○ Start each rehearsal with a quick step-by-step review of what you covered in the previous session. Consider asking your singers to present this review. This is a fantastic way to keep people on their toes and make sure that rehearsal time is spent covering new ground.

Bonus idea

Consider dividing your choir into small groups and rehearsing as mini-choirs. This will make it easier to see who needs help developing or who needs to pull their weight a little more.

Straight up!

"Does it really matter how we stand?"

Posture and alignment in singing are important. You'll be surprised by the difference good practice will make to the sound of your group, so do give it time and focus. What might feel unnatural at the start will quickly be embedded into your singers' technique.

It is important to create the right habits in your singers. It will improve their breathing technique and give them the ability to support their sound fully and bring the energy required to their singing.

Good posture:

● When standing, singers should stand in a neutral position with their feet firmly planted on the floor and their weight evenly distributed between both feet.

● Legs should be relaxed and knees should not be locked.

● The back should be broadened creating space between the shoulder blades.

● Shoulders should be relaxed and lowered.

● Arms should feel heavy and fingers loose.

● The front of the neck should be relaxed and the back of the neck should be lengthened.

● The head should be centred and not leaning to either side.

Bad posture:

● Arms folded or hands held (either in front or behind the back) can create tension in the shoulders and neck that can ultimately lead to vocal fatigue.

● Standing on one foot or slouching forward takes the whole vocal mechanism out of alignment, decreases the breath capacity and the ability to sing efficiently.

Taking it further...

Ask your choir members to stand hunched over, forcing their heads up to face forward. In this position they should sing a verse of a song that they know. When they have done this, ask them to get back into the neutral position and sing the verse again. Get them to feedback to you what effect the different posture had on their voices.

Magic ingredient no.1: The engine room

"More than anything else, I really struggle with my breathing."

Ninety per cent of all vocal problems come down to issues about breath, confusion or a lack of understanding of it, and how we should use it as singers.

Taking it further...

Experiment with a silent run-through of pieces (actually running through the piece bar-by-bar) but thinking of airflow and the importance of releasing and accepting new 'petrol' for your next phrase.

● Compare singing to an instrument. The first thing we learn about an instrument is what makes it work – how the sound is produced. Ask your singers what makes *us* work as singers. The answer is breath and air flow.

● Once they've got the idea, get them to hold the area of their body that they believe we can focus on breathing from.

● Ban the word diaphragm! We can't control it and it just creates mystery where there should be clarity. Talking about abdominal muscles instead allows singers to think about the breath process as a movement. Think about other instances where the abdominal muscles are engaged.

● Start to feel the flow of breath by breathing together simply. Free, fluid, low-set abdominal breaths are what you're looking for.

● Do not breath in and hold it – that promotes tension and constriction in the wrong area.

● Visualise your breath flow by following the journey of the air with your arms.

● Spend at least five minutes regularly in a single session resetting everyone's breathing and asking them to listen to and remind themselves of the importance of freedom of movement.

Magic ingredient no. 2: Much ado about nothing

"I don't understand why my throat and neck hurt when I sing."

Cartoons, old wives' tales and poor assumptions all lead people to think that effort, tension and focus should be directed to the throat/neck area when singing, but this is not the case. The biggest challenge is to remember that nothing happens in this area that requires physical exertion. All that is lower down the body, so it's about...nothing!

● Discuss with your singers the workings of the laryngeal area in terms of vocal activity.

● Ask them for names for this area. People will offer 'vocal cords' or 'voice box', both unhelpful and confusing phrases. Introduce the phrase 'vocal folds' as the correct term for the area involved in creating vocal sound.

● Remind them of that lovely phrase you learnt as a child – 'wind pipe' – because that is exactly how you should think about this area.

● Hammer home the point that no real effort or tension needs to be deployed to this area.

● Ask them to accept that regulated, uninterrupted air will flow through this area in order to create a healthy and efficient sound.

● Challenge them to be free and play around with smooth neck movements, slow head-shakes and personal neck massages in order to free up and remove any pointless involvement of tension.

● Get walking: sometimes when standing still and singing, the brain assumes that it needs to physically work in the wrong area and the neck becomes the centre of forced effort. So trick the brain and distract it by walking around the room, free and easy.

Bonus idea

Ask permission to place your hands on the back of the head of one of your singers as they turn their head slowly from the left and to the right (not tilting or bending). Now get people to take turns doing that while the victim is singing. Did you feel resistance or a stiffening when singing began? If the answer is yes, then work must be done to remove this obstruction.

Magic ingredient no. 3: Making faces

"I'm still not getting the sound I want from my choir. There's something missing."

A choir may have an excellent understanding of breath flow, abdominal connection, brilliantly aligned posture and physical freedom but the sound may still sound dead, and lacking in colour and quality. Surprisingly, this can be all down to their faces.

Focus first on only the face – lifting and animating the face is not just a presentation point but is also crucial for sound quality.

Involving everyone

Ask people to step out and listen to the sound. Maybe start this process with just one or two people singing so that the matched or unmatched effect can be easily heard. All this effort will make such a difference!

1. Turn your back to the choir and sing one note in two different ways: one with a fixed, dull and 'zombied' face, the second immediately after with a lifted face, switched on cheeks and animated eyes. The first approach should produce a dull and colourless sound with little projection, buzz or resonance, while the second should produce a bright and resonant sound, alive and energised. Ask the choir to highlight the differences and choose which they prefer – with any luck they'll say number two!

2. Now instruct the choir to repeat this experiment themselves, listening for any change in tone and thinking about how it feels to sing with their faces in different positions.

If an audience can't hear the words being offered by the singers in front of them, they are even further away from the most important overall factor – the music. Vowel sounds are especially important to think about when trying to create a focused, resonant sound. When you have several voices singing together, it is important for everyone to focus on matching their vowel sounds to each other to allow the note and its quality to shine through.

○ Practise singing focused vowel sounds together, concentrating on achieving a bright resonance, to let the note 'ping'. Make sure the singers are supporting the notes throughout, so that they don't lose their focused sound.

○ When we sing, we can't see our mouths and the sound we're producing, so it can be helpful to use imagery. One useful image to keep in mind is a focused beam of light, like a spotlight.

○ Imagine a theatre light, a standard 'profile' light with four 'flaps'. Those flaps are called barn-doors and they're used to focus the light into one position. A singer's lips and tongue are the barn-doors and focus the vowel in the same way, so this is a brilliant way to visualise vowel positions and how we send out sound like a ray of light towards a specific point.

○ You could use your hands to help visualise the beam of light. Come up with some hand signals for each vowel sound, to help match your vowel sounds together.

Top tip

Come back to this crucial step all the time, it will take many rehearsals before everyone understands and realises the importance of matching every vowel. Take care that the vowels don't lose focus when the pitch changes.

Breathing, breathing, breathing

"I feel like a broken record, but I still don't think I've got everyone breathing correctly."

It is normal to spend a lot of time talking about breathing, and it's important that you do. No matter what level your choir is at, no matter how much you've spoken about it, you shouldn't stop.

Top tip

There is a fairly common technical exercise that asks singers to breathe in, then hold their breath and then breathe out. This doesn't assist or improve any part of the process, and can promote laryngeal tension and rigid fold positions, so don't do it!

○ Consider spending a full rehearsal on breathing.

○ Create a chart or image of the vocal issues that people experience and ask your singers to contribute to this.

○ Try and find a few videos that look at vocal fold movement and phonation, and show these to your singers.

○ Find some videos that show the intercostal movements within the body during breath movement. Visual aids will be extremely useful for your singers to help them understand the problems more clearly.

○ Be careful of the terminology you use and avoid any confusion. Deep breath, big breath, suck in, and push air should be avoided when instructing your singers. Air should never be forced – it should be very natural.

○ Encourage singers to accept air into their lungs as they would when they yawn. It should feel a relaxing movement, not at all forced.

○ A very good question to ask is, 'How did that feel?'

Words, words, words

"Audiences in row three backwards always tell me they can't hear the words in performances."

No matter how good your singers are or how many times you have covered the issue, you'll always find that the overall choral diction can be improved. Remind singers that there is no strength in numbers regarding clarity of words. More than one singer singing the same words makes it less audible to the audience.

Instrumentalists are able to articulate their sounds with physical actions that are very tangible and singers sometimes forget that they can too – it's all down to the consonants.

❍ Remind your singers that if they feel like they are going over the top on diction and pronunciation, they are only just doing enough.

❍ Consider consonants to be the trigger in your gun, directing the vowels to fly like bullets with power and precision.

❍ Encourage your singers to engage their abdomen and breath to achieve this and empower their consonant production. Be careful that your singers don't tense and 'grip' their larynx when trying to achieve this.

❍ Speak your music to a whisper, focusing on consonant production.

❍ Your singers may know the lyrics so well that they forget audiences are hearing it for the first time. Remind the choir that it's their duty to tell the story.

Involving everyone

Send one or two singers to the back of the venue during your rehearsals to be 'diction wardens'. It's far more supportive to have fellow choir members feeding back than your singers hearing you on repeat.

Emotional extras

"My choir sing all the right notes but they don't show any emotion in the songs."

Getting your choir to sing with emotion is absolutely essential if you want to move your audience. Singing a melody and some lyrics may sound nice but it's not going to blow anyone away, however accurate. Remember, your singers are there to tell a story that your audience should enjoy, feel, relate to or sympathise with. Understand the real meaning behind the songs by encouraging your singers to tap into their own memories and journeys.

Taking it further...

Ask your choir members to listen to songs where the performer clearly expresses a raw, undeniable emotion. Songs like Michael Jackson's *She's Out of My Life* is a great example. He cries at the end of the song and sings a few wrong notes. The performance embodies a true 'mature' emotion. The listener feels Jackson's pain and empathises with this moment of vulnerability.

Your thoughts and the way you feel will come across in your singing. It is therefore vital that each choir member must know what the song is about before they sing it. With each song, make sure you spend time discussing the meaning of the song with the choir. There are many different types of songs: songs of hope, happiness, love, sadness, pride, weakness or empowerment, to name a few. Most singers, to varying degrees, will have had a sense of these emotions before. Use some exercises to try and tease these emotions out:

1. Read through the lyrics as a group and discuss which emotion the writer of the song is trying to convey. Ask each member to find a space in the room and think of a memory that embodies that particular feeling. They should each work alone and try to ignore everyone else (three minutes).

2. Walking around the room, they should relive that memory, focusing on the most poignant part, while allowing their body to express that emotion or energy (three minutes).

3. Read through the lyrics again. Looking at the words, the singers should continue to walk around the space while the song is playing. They should use their memory to immerse themselves in the narrative of the song. This is now *their* story and not the story of the writer any more (five minutes).

4. It might be helpful to write down or discuss any feelings associated with this emotion as a group. This should be encouraged but not demanded.

5. Perform the song, focusing only on the emotional connection. Encourage the singers to be true to their feelings without too much emphasis on the vocal quality to begin with.

6. Once the emotional connection is there, the singers can start to bring back the vocal quality.

You may find there are some moments when a singer will fully connect to an emotion and be overcome by that feeling. Allow this to happen. It will help to make it honest and believable. You will not need to do this exercise every time you learn a new piece. Once the choir get into the habit of connecting to the song, it will eventually become easier and quicker for them to do so.

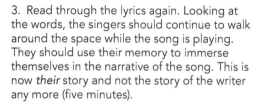

Involving everyone

Watch Pavarotti's last and final performance of *Nessun Dorma* at the opening of the Turin Winter Olympics, months before he passed away. Even though Pavarotti wasn't singing live, with his physical strength fading he gives a performance embodying emotion that moves.

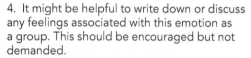

Ensemble skills

"I know we've got concerts and events coming up, but this year I just want to focus on making my choir tighter, more responsive and musically efficient."

It's quite simple really. The more you rehearse and sing together, the better your choir will be.

Involving everyone

The week after your next concert, come together and review the pieces. Before giving any of your own feedback, ask the singers what they thought. What did they feel were the strengths and weaknesses? Be hypercritical and take it on board for the next project.

◗ Insist on a quiet and respectful room and introduce a rehearsal etiquette.

◗ Ensure that people are quiet in the first few seconds after you stop a section to work on it. These moments are the most crucial – if singers start chatting, it breaks the focus and they'll miss your comments.

◗ Memorising music helps your choir to really understand and learn the song to the highest level. Everyone can then put their full energy into listening and watching. If choirs listen and watch, they will sing as one.

◗ Breath together – starting each song with everyone breathing at the same time and pace launches the piece on a path to precision.

◗ Don't settle for 80% accuracy, if you've highlighted an issue and asked for some change or improvement and it doesn't entirely happen, go back and keep covering it until it is correct. Don't settle for 'That'll do, I guess'.

◗ Contact a professional choir or vocal group and ask if you (or your entire choir) could go and respectfully observe one of their rehearsals. You'll learn so much about etiquette and ensemble precision just by watching and listening.

◗ Sometimes, ask your choir why they think you're still working on a section, or ask them to highlight exactly what needs to change to improve a passage.

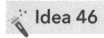

In or out (of tune)

"Tuning is my choir's Achilles' heel."

Tuning often comes down to one question: do your singers listen to each other? If you sing in tune, audiences return, new members arrive and good reviews are gained. Singing out of tune, however complex your music or excellent your singers, will have the opposite effect.

○ Try 'scrambling' (see Idea 21). This is perhaps the single most powerful way to correct tuning.

○ Sing things quietly to a hum, an 'oo', or a unified vowel which allows singers to hear the harmony clearly. Relentlessly forced dynamics can have a negative effect and push the line sharp or flat.

○ Tonal centreing. Tuning can be improved by increasing your singers' awareness of where their part is in relation to the key note.

○ Listen! Ask the whole group to listen around them more when singing, both to people on other parts and on their own.

○ Vowel placement and pronunciation. Discrepancies in vowels can make things sound out of tune when they're not far off. Ensure vowels are placed correctly and consistently across the choir.

○ Go naked! Your choir's relationship with tuning and tonality will improve dramatically if they are not always supported by an accompaniment, so try singing a cappella.

○ Work with individuals. Sometimes there are one or two singers whose shaky tuning causes everything to wobble. This can be difficult, but tackle it head-on. Meet with them on their own to work on security of line and try and get to the bottom of the problem.

Taking it further...

There are many more factors at work in how to get your choir locked in tune. Learn more about pressed airflow, poor alignment and facial energy and explore correcting these with your choir.

Bonus idea

Robert Isaacs from the USA has introduced a brilliant idea called 'The Magic Pattern'. In its simplest form, it is assigning numbers to the degrees of the scale and referencing your accuracy with respect to 'one' as you go.

A cappella

"I wouldn't dare sing a song without accompaniment. That is far too difficult."

A cappella music is a very exposing genre for a choir and is far less forgiving of mistakes. You not only have to make sure you are singing all the right notes and words, but you must create a balance across the harmony, instrumental and percussive parts and stay in tune. It is a tough genre for a choir which started with accompaniment, but there are ways to help with this.

Here is an idea for exploring a cappella for the first time. Don't take this seriously, make it a fun exercise and allow the choir to make some weird and wonderful sounds and get into the swing of singing without any musical accompaniment.

Taking it further...

Choose three people to sing the vocal parts and get the rest of the choir to explore singing the accompanying parts.

● Sing a song that you already have in your repertoire with accompaniment or use something like *Lean on Me* in a simple choral arrangement with a backing track.

● Pick out the various parts within the song covered by the accompaniment: the bassline, the drums, the melody, the harmonies. What other instruments can the singers pick out? Is there a brass section? Strings? Is there a guitar solo?

● Separate the singers and ask small groups to choose one of those parts and work on singing it.

● Come back into a group, try to put the parts together with the accompaniment, and see what comes out.

● Repeat the process, but provide a skeletal bass line or occasional chords to support the singers.

● Now take away the accompaniment and see how it holds together. Staying in key is a crucial element to make this genre a success, so make sure you know which key you are starting in and take care during any modulations.

Part 5
Group dynamics

Location, location, implication

"Well I wouldn't normally go to a choral concert, but this venue they're performing in looks so cool."

Getting the concert venue right is so important for both your choir and your audience. Ask yourself what you want from a venue and how it will enhance all your hard work and make an impact on your audience.

Taking it further...

If a great venue has a price tag, be brave and think about any organisations which would like to see a concert happen there and might sponsor you.

Bonus idea

Make sure that the venue's logo, website and box office number are clearly visible on your flyers. Try and get the venue involved in the PR of your performance – it may help to sell your tickets to its own network.

❀ Consider your repertoire. What you're singing has a huge impact on where you should perform it – a cappella early choral music will need a good amount of acoustic reverberation, but when instruments and amplification are involved the sound will need to be drier.

❀ A unique and interesting venue can sometimes make or break your performance and represent a deciding factor as to whether people actually decide to attend. Furthermore, a unique and interesting venue can make a huge difference to how your singers sing. The sights and sounds are as important for them as the audience. Be brave, be bold and remember – a choir is the most mobile and malleable of any performing ensemble, so the world is your oyster. Take advantage of this.

❀ Speak to your local council's events department to see if they can introduce you to some unusual venues or free spaces. Consider venues such as museums, tunnels, car parks and warehouses. As long as you've got permission and the conditions are suitable for your choir and audience, why not?

❀ Appoint a concerts manager from within your choir. This will take so much stress away from you and allow you to focus on what you do best, the music. Get your concerts manager to join you on a site visit to the concert venue and assess how the logistics would work on the day.

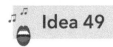
Rows, and blocks ... YAWN!

"I absolutely loved how that group had so many staging formations during the concert."

Thinking outside the box about how you place your singers in a performance space can make a huge difference to the success of a gig for everyone involved.

● Consider your repertoire and close your eyes. Imagine a music video for each piece, think about how you would imagine singers standing if rows were banned. Then go and make it happen!

● Have fun forming your choir into many different shapes: circles, diamonds, hollow squares, etc.

● Try different staging options in rehearsals as a trial. It will certainly lift the atmosphere and make for a special session.

● Work out where you need to be to conduct, or whether you're needed at all!

● Use the space. Don't be afraid to abandon the stage. You can use aisles, balconies and any other available space that you can see. It might affect lighting and mean you need to sing from memory, but it will be worth it.

● If the singers are all over the space, agree on a focus spot where they look, and don't have this directly into the audience unless appropriate.

Make sure that the ideas you adopt don't compromise your core sound and what you are trying to achieve musically. Good staging should highlight the artistic excellence, not detract from it.

Anecdote

Some of the most memorable concerts I've ever been part of have been those that kept the audience in continuous suspense about where we were going next. Don't be afraid of your ideas!

Dom

Bonus idea

Surrounding your audience in a circle can be hugely effective. It allows them to get up-close and personal and be immersed in your music.

Stamina for the show

"We always have loads of energy during rehearsals, but then when I get to the concerts my choir seem so exhausted and always unable to deliver what I know they can!"

An important thing to remember during rehearsals is that your choir will need to be prepared both physically and mentally for the concert. Concerts are more demanding than rehearsals and if you want the best out of your singers you will need to make sure they have built up the stamina to last through a full concert.

Top tip

As part of your final run, why not ask your singers to grade their performance so that they identify the areas they need to watch out for in the concert?

○ Refer to the concert frequently. Constantly remind singers what they are working towards.

○ Stopping and starting when going through songs is inevitable as you refine sections, but try to limit this.

○ Ensure that you regularly run your pieces from start to finish, no matter how scrappy the singing or notes. You'll find that some issues are resolved by the singers themselves, and more importantly you will build up the choir's stamina for that piece and awareness of how much effort is involved.

○ Programme your concert order carefully, thinking not just in terms of the music but also in terms of vocal health and expenditure. If there are challenging or long pieces, don't place them towards the end when the singers won't have the energy to tackle them.

○ Follow a difficult piece with something easier.

○ Make sure that whenever possible you have a rehearsal in the concert venue and run through all pieces. New acoustics come with a whole range of challenges and problems and the singers need time to adjust.

○ Remind your singers to be fully rested for the concert day – arriving after a good night's sleep, fed and watered.

The final countdown

"No matter how much we prepare, we never really get things correct in the last rehearsal, and then we go on stage terrified."

It is common for the rehearsal before the concert to get a little out of hand. There are a lot of nerves and excitement floating about and it's easy to get side tracked. Consider the following tips to ensure that everything runs smoothly.

○ Be strict with yourself. Sit down a few days before your performance and create a detailed rehearsal plan. Hand this schedule out to everyone so that they know exactly what will happen on the day. Some conductors do a minute-by-minute timetable to make sure everything is covered as needed.

○ Some people like to run the programme in order while others run it in reverse. Choose the order which is best for you – but if there is a piece that is exhausting to sing and would therefore benefit from a slot earlier, do that.

○ Run through all of the material. A lot of things will be solved just by giving your singers the opportunity to feel the music in the new space.

○ Appoint someone to help with time management and ensure you follow your schedule.

○ Use appropriate warm-ups. Your choir may be full of nervous energy, so make the first activity instil calm. A slow and methodical warm-up is best and using an energetic physical warm-up just before they go on stage for the concert will get their pulse racing and body fizzing in the right way.

○ Don't work your choir too hard and rehearse too much. Concert days are usually long and drawn out, so pace yourself and your choir.

○ Keep both yourself and your choir well fed and hydrated, and allow plenty of breaks.

Bonus idea

Take a group photo on concert day to archive the event and share on social media.

Off by heart or from the dots?

"One of the pieces in our last concert was a piece that the choir have been doing for years, and a lot of people didn't have copies of the music on the concert day so we decided to do that piece from memory. The sound suddenly changed and it ended up being the best moment in the concert."

Have you ever stopped to wonder why the moment you put something in someone's hand you lose their focus, and the object steals it? Whenever possible, be bold and get material learnt so well that your singers are set free by singing from memory.

○ Explain to your singers how the overall sound and ensemble quality increases when they just focus on you, their singing, and listening to those around them.

○ Teach them something simple without music and assess how easy things were in terms of sound and ability to focus on you and the way you are crafting the sound.

○ Agree collectively on a few items in your repertoire or next programme that you could perform from memory. Don't pile on the pressure – let this be a joint decision.

○ Let singers know that the responsibility is on them to learn it. Give only a small amount of time to memory work in practice sessions.

○ Don't be afraid if it falls to pieces. That's great – better in rehearsal than the gig!

○ Set the choir a formal deadline for when they need to have their parts learned.

Bonus idea

The benefit of building a repertoire of memorised pieces is that the group becomes more adaptable and versatile. It will help you perform in unusual places where lighting and holding music is impractical, and encores are at your fingertips.

Lord of the dance

My choir members are so rigid on stage. How can I get them moving?"

In the same way that varying the position of the choir stimulates the visual as well as the aural senses, dancing and movement can add to a concert experience. Many choirs shy away from this as it takes them away from their comfort zone. With these simple ideas you can start to get your choir loosened up for the challenge.

Dancing can remove inhibitions, which may be restricting your singers not just physically but also vocally and in their self-expression. Even if you don't dance in concert, it may be exactly what you need in rehearsal.

◐ The energy and the initiative has to come from you as the leader. Start simply and pick a few simple moves to do during a chorus – a step, click or a sway from side to side. Do these moves while conducting and encourage the choir to follow.

◐ As a game, pick a piece the singers know well and ask them to move any way they choose throughout the whole song while singing. If they stop, they are out. This is a fun way to allow choir members to get comfortable with using their bodies while performing a song.

◐ Form a circle facing outwards and play an upbeat song. Each singer takes it in turn to step into the circle and dance as if nobody's watching. This can be developed by gradually allowing more and more people to face inwards and watch while people dance. It should ultimately be a very liberating feeling, but it's not easy being asked to reveal yourself in this way, so be patient and sensitive.

Bonus idea ★

Very simple movements can have dramatic effects – starting with backs turned to the audience and each part turning around just before they sing, or ending a concert by walking out and letting the sound fade gradually.

Idea 54

Over to you

"Our audiences are always so much fun. How can I involve them more?"

Audience participation in performances is fantastic. No matter what audience you find yourself in front of, there will be some people who will want to sing too, so do make time for this. Not only is this a fun exercise for them but it gives your choir a break.

A simple way is to teach your audience their own part of a song in your programme:

○ Include a feel-good song in your programme. Choose one with simple lyrics that has a melody that is easy to learn.

○ Announce to the audience that you will be asking them to sing along in at least one of the songs that you are performing.

○ Before that song, run through the part that the audience is to join in with.

○ If you are brave enough to challenge your audience to sing in harmony then quickly rehearse this with the audience too.

○ Bring the audience in at the right time during the song – just a chorus or repeated refrain is plenty to make them feel involved.

In a Christmas concert you can easily use well-known carols to punctuate your concert and allow people to participate. Carols won't need teaching and could provide a good start, middle and end point to programmes. Just pick ones that are widely known (not just your favourites) and ask everyone to stand and join in.

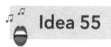

Sharing the spotlight

"The same people always do the solos – how can I change this?"

Choosing soloists in a choir can be a difficult prospect if you don't have many strong singers to choose from and have singers who are very keen but not yet able. It can be tricky to get the balance right. Here are some things to consider.

● If you have a lot of capable singers, audition them for solo parts. This can be done in private or in front of the choir, and gives you a great knowledge of who is keen to take solo parts.

● Distribute the solos evenly between those who are capable, and don't stick rigidly to one soloist per song – change the soloists for the same piece regularly.

● Where an octave change is workable, consider mixing up the female and male solos.

● Suggest additional singing lessons for singers who need some additional input before being given a solo.

● Pair stronger soloists with those who are developing, for guidance.

● If there is a single solo in a piece, can you break it up so that more singers can get involved? Where the verses are solos, you could give different verses to different singers.

● Encourage developing singers by giving them performances that won't expose them, or semichorus parts (where a few solo singers sing a part together).

Taking it further...

Having more than one soloist per song is a smart move, otherwise a concert can become insecure if a single person is unwell and can't make it. Distributing the responsibility is key to the growth of the singers and the musical stability of the choir.

Looking good

"I'm not sure why but my singers never seem to look good on stage – and it's not their outfits."

Looking good on stage is a must, and it's not just about clothing, hair, and make-up, but posture, facial expressions and the overall performance energy. This can make audiences tune in or switch off – and we know which we want!

People in choirs often look a little scared. It may be that they are under-rehearsed or that the sense of occasion is too much for them, and this can lead to strange facial expressions. Remind singers that the key to them looking good is not their clothing but their overall presence – they must captivate audiences and draw them towards the music.

You have to work to get your choir ready for their performances in all ways, and looking good is part of this. There is nothing more off-putting for an audience than scared faces that are unable to hide their immediate feelings and fully enter into their performance. Consider the following:

Taking it further...

What happens in between pieces? If you are moving position, or leaving the stage, or just standing still, think about how this can be tidy and neat.

● What does the audience see? Stage a mock performance and video it to show your singers how they look when they perform. Once they become their own audience, any fidgeting, scared faces or vacant expressions will be clear to see. Note what needs to be improved. Your performance as the conductor is important, too – even though the audience may mostly see your back, do you also look confident and engaged? Lead by example.

● What does the rehearsal conductor see? Using mirrors can help choirs work through issues immediately during the rehearsal and start to smile, move in time, stand still or move in the correct way. Can you find a dance studio that has a mirrored wall?

● Invite a crowd. Inviting people in regularly to impromptu performances is a great way for your choir members to get feedback that is not from you and get used to singing for others as a matter of course. Doing this regularly will increase singers' confidence and make them ready for public performances really quickly. You may get some new recruits too!

● Create the illusion. Looking confident on stage is sometimes an act, and singers need to know that however they feel, they must go on stage and convey the story of the music to the audience. Your choir will get into the swing of things after a while, but in the meantime you can direct their facial expressions, posture and movement to create the right effect. This should become more organic and natural over time, but don't be afraid to ask people to put on an act – it's a performance.

● Start at the very beginning and think about the end. Looking good starts from the first time your audience sees you and lasts until you leave, so make sure you have thought through how you enter and leave the performance space, walk, and hold music (if relevant).

What to wear

"My choir has been wearing the same outfit for the last five years. What should I do to mix things up?"

What to wear on stage can be a never-ending discussion, as everyone will have different ideas and personal styles. Here are some basic rules to follow when choosing what to wear.

Taking it further...

Having a few outfits can be useful for tailoring the choir's appearance to different occasions and seasons.

Top tip

Allowing everyone to be an individual generally works well. There will be times when you need everyone wearing the same thing, but dressing for performances can feel much less of a burden for singers if they can dress comfortably within some simple parameters.

● Comfort: make sure outfits are comfortable to wear and will not restrict movement. Fit is important too – constant adjustment during a performance will distract both singers and audience.

● Know your style: what type of choir are you? Does a classic choir robe work for you or are you more of a contemporary choir which would look better in jeans and trainers? Choose outfits that are appropriate for the ages of the people within your choir.

● Brand it: clothing that links to your brand is a good way of giving your choir a unique feel and style. Consider putting your choir name and logo on a top that can be worn in performance.

● Uniformity: look like a group made of individuals. A strict colour theme like pastels, monochrome or all-grey can then be given flexibility by letting members decide on their style within this.

● Add a splash of colour. A single colour can be used as an accent in whatever way singers choose: tie, shirt, scarf, top, hair accessory or other item of their choice.

● Freshen up the old: If you already have a set uniform that works, adding accessories will give it a new lease of life. Make this consistent across the choir – red jewellery or white neck scarves, and perhaps change for each concert.

Let there be light

"I always feel I could make more of an impact visually in my concerts, but I'm not quite sure how."

A simple way to increase the visual impact of a performance is to look into lighting options.

○ As part of your concert venue site visit, check whether the venue has adequate lighting. Take the time of your concert into consideration so that you think about how much natural lighting there will be – will your singers and any musicians be able to see their music adequately?

○ See whether the venue has any spotlights or a lighting desk, and whether you can use them without additional cost. Can the venue show you how to operate the lighting or provide someone with expertise? If not, get in touch with a local lighting firm, theatrical provider or hire company and get some prices.

○ Think about colours. Splashes of coloured light are very simple to achieve and can lift the performance. The equipment is easy to source. Find some photos or videos of choral performances which use limited lighting to great effect.

○ Simple LED lights that have a variety of colour options are easy to set up and can be placed subtly on the floor behind the performers to augment the backdrop.

○ If this is too technical, consider candles a winter concert by candlelight is loved by most audiences.

Bonus idea

Look at connecting with a local college or university that offers theatrical, lighting or staging courses. It might welcome the opportunity to collaborate on a project as part of its students' practical experience.

I can hear music

"We worked so hard during rehearsals, but just before the concert started our sound system failed and our show was a disaster!"

Your audience is there to hear wonderful music and you have worked long and hard to produce it. If the sound isn't as intended or members of the audience can't hear, it is frustrating for everyone. Be sure that the logistics and levels are right and avoid any sudden complications on gig day.

● Always allow time for a soundcheck. Get your choir singing and move around the building and listen from various positions. Check you are hearing the balance you want.

● If your choir is singing with just the natural acoustic to carry the sound, are singers stood in the right position within the venue to be heard by everyone? A simple shuffle forward may be needed, or to move the soloists closer to the audience. Do certain voice parts need to be nearer the front than others?

● If your choir is amplified, are the microphones at the right levels for the size of the venue?

● Have you a recorded accompaniment? Does it need to be played from CD or mp3, and does the recording work?

● Can the accompaniment be heard by both the choir and the audience without drowning out the singers?

● Do you need a microphone to speak to the audience? Make sure there is one close to your conducting position, that you know how to switch it on, and that a sound technician knows you might use it.

🎤 Part 6
In concert

Choosing repertoire

"There is so much music out there. How do I choose the right material?"

Unless you are writing music specially for your choir, you will need to choose choral pieces or arrangements that suit the voices and ability of the choir. There are lots of resources for this, so it shouldn't be difficult to source some great things, but think carefully to get the best out of your choir.

Taking it further...

Experiment with writing your own music and arrangements. You know exactly what your singers can do and you can write to their strengths. Start simply, and don't be afraid to ask someone to help and guide you.

○ Choose material that the choir believes in and that complements the choir's ethos. If your singers can relate to what they are singing, a lot of the aspects of excellent performance will be easier to achieve.

○ Be challenging but not damaging! Start with some simple pieces which you are confident your choir can tackle, but add some items that stretch and take the group out of its comfort zones.

○ Think about whether the vocal ranges of a particular piece suit your choir (see Idea 61).

○ Consider your audience. What kind of audiences do you tend to attract, and what music do they respond to? Try and keep your audience happy while also introducing them to some material which broadens their listening experience.

○ Unless you are targeting a very specific audience, try to stay away from pieces with lyrics that are not child-friendly or could offend.

○ Go to concerts and listen to recordings of other choirs – broaden your own knowledge of appropriate repertoire.

○ Attend a training day where you can sing through lots of new music and get new ideas.

Picking good vocal ranges

"I've found some fantastic repertoire and got the choir really excited, but it's always too low or too high for someone. How can I make everyone happy?"

You can present a well-rehearsed performance with excellent technical grounding, brilliant presentation and a varied and interesting programme, but if the ranges don't match that of your choir the performance will sound strained and probably go out of tune.

● Most mixed voice choirs are pretty versatile and cover a large vocal range between them. If there are passages that are too high or too low, see if you can cover the part using singers from a different voice part.

● Commission pieces and arrangements to be written for your group. A lot of choirs have conductors or leaders who arrange for them, because a bespoke arrangement can play to a group's strengths.

● If you would prefer to arrange without a score, get to grips with recording software. This will enable you to record yourself singing each individual part, and work out your arrangement without the pressure of notating. Apple's GarageBand is very user-friendly and good for this.

● If you would like to score your arrangements, get to grips with a notation software which will enable you to listen back to your arrangement and edit it as you write it.

● Know the comfortable ranges of your voice parts and take time to find the right repertoire. When buying music, visit a shop with a large range and spend a good amount of time looking through the entire piece before buying it. If it gets quite high for your singers, check it's in a part where you have strength in numbers.

Involving everyone

There might be some choir members who write music and would relish the opportunity to hear their material performed by the choir. Can you create an opportunity for them to get involved in this way?

Idea 62

Notation or not?

"My choir has never really used scores and many members don't read music, but I want to broaden our horizons and work from printed music. Should I go for it?"

There are advantages and disadvantages to working with sheet music. Some choirs use sheet music and others don't. Both ways are absolutely valid and involve different skills. Whatever your choir does, why not try the opposite?

○ If you are introducing sheet music to your choir, start with something simple.

○ Even if no one in your choir reads music, don't be afraid to hand out sheet music to everyone. With the help of the lyrics, you'll be surprised how much singers can follow.

○ Benefits of choirs working from sheet music are many. Composers and arrangers mark subtleties and accents in their scores which may not be adopted just by listening. Singers can also see visually how their part interacts with others and can mark notes on the music to jog their memory in rehearsal and performance.

○ If you want to move away from the dots and teach things by ear, start simply and repeat phrases over and over – repetition is the mother of excellence! Make sure all demonstrations are clear and accurate.

○ Being free of sheet music means your singers can solely focus on you, their singing and their colleagues. It fine-tunes their aural memory skills as they have to be relied upon completely.

○ Use both approaches in tandem: introduce your music without notation, cover all the elements and then hand out the music.

Bonus idea

Along with introducing your choir to music reading, provide singers with musicianship training. Approach large youth choirs, Music Hubs, universities and choral associations and see if they can support you. Could a tutor come to your choir and lead a session?

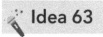

Why bother singing a cappella?

"Singing a cappella seemed very daunting, but my choir have developed so much as musicians since we started singing without an accompaniment."

Singing unaccompanied can be very daunting as it leaves the choir very exposed, but there are so many advantages to doing so. Your singers will not only develop their voices but their overall musicianship will improve as well.

Top tip

Start with the simplest of repertoire in a couple of parts. The most important thing is that you are listening to each other and working as a single unit.

❍ Working a cappella means that you are not bound by any particular arrangement and so you could consider arranging or devising some pieces on your own. Try creating something yourselves from scratch.

❍ You can move the key up or down slightly to suit your singers without complex transposition of accompaniments.

❍ Your singers will become better at listening to each other and responding to sounds around them. Get them to close their eyes when they sing to fully absorb the sound of their combined, unaccompanied voices.

❍ Without a guiding accompaniment, the singers will develop their internal pulse.

❍ The choir will enjoy providing the whole harmonic interest and hearing how it contributes to that.

❍ Singers will also need to develop their ear to stay in key and will need to improve their pitch accuracy.

❍ Duplicating instrumental backing and drum beats is something that many singers won't have tried before. It will be a new, fun and challenging experience for them and will really help to develop their musical ear.

Idea 64

Turn up the volume

"Why do you need so many mics?"

With some venues it's easy to work out whether amplification is needed – but solve the problem as simply as possible to enable your sound and music to be heard in the way you intend.

Do a venue visit and establish where the choir will sing from. Some event organisers like to get creative with where they place a choir without considering how the sound will carry. Check that the placement will work for everyone involved.

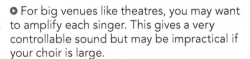

Bonus idea

If the event organiser says that there is no PA provision, make it clear that the choir may not be heard and try to ensure the choir sings from a place where voices have the best chance of carrying.

- For big venues like theatres, you may want to amplify each singer. This gives a very controllable sound but may be impractical if your choir is large.

- If you have a big choir, the sound may fill the venue but you may need a microphone for soloists.

- A few simple overhead microphones will amplify the whole choir without pulling out any individual voices. This is best for most classical repertoire.

- You could select a few voices to close-mic and have overhead mics for the rest of the choir. This is a good way of getting your choir heard without too much effort.

- In venues which are created especially for vocal music (e.g. churches) the architecture may do all the hard work for you.

- Do you have an accompaniment which needs amplification regardless of your singers' needs?

- In a dry space like a carpeted room or outdoors, amplification may be essential to ensure you are heard.

The world's a stage

"We have been rehearsing for a while now but we haven't had any performances."

Any choir will need to seek out opportunities to show off the hard work in rehearsal to an audience. This is key to keeping your members motivated and focused.

Performances don't have to be events that take lots of organisation and, while you may wait for the musical director of the latest West End show to come calling, there are lots of opportunities for choirs to perform at smaller local venues. These include the local supermarket, train stations, coffee shops or shopping centres. They may not seem like prestigious venues to perform in, but you have a captive audience who would love to hear some great singing, you might pick up new recruits, and you might be heard by people who subsequently want to book you. Approaching these places involves nothing more than a phone call. It might be a good idea to try these venues around the Christmas period when it is busy and people are expecting some singers. Once you have a relationship with the venue manager, you can then ask for performances at other times of the year.

Bonus idea

Start by offering your services for free. Once people know how good you are and what they can expect when booking you, consider charging a fee or expenses.

Local events such as fun days, community events, fundraising events and religious festivals are great opportunities to get performing in the area where you live. If the event is outdoors, remember to think about amplification (even if your choir is not normally amplified, voices outside are easily lost) but the venue or event might already have this organised for their other events.

Checkmate!

"I always feel totally overwhelmed. On top of rehearsals, I'm either recruiting new members, booking the next concert, programming the music or promoting the choir, and I always end up missing something."

Don't forget the importance of delegating. Pass on some of the responsibility to trusted and passionate people from within your choir, and create a detailed project checklist for each project or concert.

Create a master calendar of all your events for the whole year. Once you have your calendar, create a checklist for every project, working backwards from the concert day.

1. Concert day: final rehearsal in venue and concert.

2. Two days before concert: rehearsal in venue.

3. Seven days before concert: confirm times, equipment and plans with the venue.

4. One month before concert: big push to promote your concert, with press, social media and flyers.

5. Three months before concert: tickets available for sale.

6. Three months before concert: begin rehearsals for the event.

7. Four months before concert: poster completed and concert up on your website and social media pages.

8. Five months before concert: deadline for ordering music and hiring equipment.

9. Six months before concert: deadline for theme and repertoire.

10. Twelve months before concert: book a venue.

11. Twelve months before concert: book choir members for concert and rehearsal dates.

Bonus idea

Use a Doodle poll or another way to clarify the availability of your singers before you book all your concerts, tours and events far in advance – this will give you the best chance of having your full complement of singers.

Part 7
Not just concerts

Smart recording

"I want to record my choir but I don't have any recording equipment."

The advantage of having recordings of your choir is that you can show off what you've been working on to family and friends, and use them as demos to promote yourselves.

Involving everyone

If you don't have the technology or this still sounds daunting, you will almost certainly have someone in your choir who will be happy to help you. Don't be afraid to ask.

● Find a good recording space. Your rehearsal space is probably the best place to start as it's familiar, but make sure that there isn't any outside noise that will leak in.

● Use smartphones. Using as many smartphones as you have, mount them on tripods with mics pointing towards your singers. You may have to experiment a few times with this to get the volume right. The louder the choir, the higher the chance the recordings will distort.

● Record everyone together. It is often beneficial for all parts to sing at the same time, but place a few smartphones in front of each section. Try to start the phones recording at the same time as it will make it easier for you in the mixing process.

● Gather the recordings. Ask your singers to email you the recordings from their phone. Ensure that they label them first!

● Mix them, using some sequencing software like Audacity, GarageBand or Logic, and import all the tracks. Get the right balance between parts. You will have to line them up a little to make sure that all are in time with one another.

● Add some effects to give it a bit of sheen.

● Et voilà! You have a good-quality, easy-to-make, cheap recording.

Singing for weird events

"I've been asked to sing at the zoo, around the animals. How should I prepare?"

Singing at weird events can be challenging, but also fun. Consider the following when making preparations for any unconventional events.

● Site visit, site visit, site visit! Going into an event blind on the day is risky, to say the least. If it isn't possible to actually visit the venue, then try to get as much information as possible, including pictures, staging plans, and size of the venue.

● How loud should you be? You don't want to be too loud for an event that just requires background music, or too quiet to be heard if you are the main act. Find out in advance whether there will be a sound team available to amplify you and help you on the day.

● Is the performance area well lit? You may be required to sing behind curtains, on balconies, or anywhere else the organisers decide. You must make sure that there is enough light for you all to see.

● Will the choir need to move while singing, or during the performance? Be sure to work out where the choir will need to move from and to, and if possible practise this beforehand.

● Brief the singers as fully as possible – it is important for them to know what to expect.

Anecdote

Once my choir was asked to perform at an open-air event at a zoo, which was wonderful. However, we were told not to be too loud as it might scare the lions! We had to sing at less than half the usual volume and the lions loved it. Of course they did! The luxury was that we had a good sound team on the day who were very good at balancing the sound between us and the backing tracks.

Mark

Idea 69

Embrace your inner YouTube

"I could never put anything on YouTube! We're not good enough."

YouTube is an extremely useful tool not just in promoting and exposing your choir, but also as a way of keeping your rehearsals focused and documented. Millions of people watch YouTube videos every day and you can make use of this mighty force by adding a video to the mix.

Members may feel they don't have the ability to make a good YouTube video, but this should encourage them to raise their game. The first time, it could be delivered as a surprise challenge, but ultimately you want to get to a place where you're ready to share your music at any time.

Top tip

If you're nervous about doing this, start by making the videos private. When both you and the choir become more comfortable with being filmed, start making videos public.

- Setup a YouTube channel.
- Choose a suitable song that your choir enjoys singing.
- Get hold of a video camera or just use a smartphone.
- Surprise the choir at the next rehearsal with this task.
- Run through your song and then press record.
- Post it to your YouTube channel.
- Select whether the video is private or public.

Remember that the point of this exercise is not to promote your choir, but to focus the rehearsal and give it clear direction, keep singers focused and performing to their best.

Singing lessons

"I brought in a singing teacher, who has been working with our singers for a few years now. The difference it's made to my choir is amazing."

Aim to develop your singers' voices by encouraging them to take a few singing lessons. This doesn't have to take up any more of their time – it can be done within a rehearsal.

○ Get in touch with singing teachers you may know and ask if they would be interested in providing some tuition, both individually as well as to the group.

○ Encourage your singers to take at least two one-to-one lessons of 30 minutes each year.

○ Make sure there is a suitable space within your rehearsal venue for these lessons to take place, as ideally they should run simultaneously with your rehearsals, with people just excusing themselves as they need to.

○ Inform your singers of the benefits of taking lessons. You could look at the possibility of trying to apply for a grant for this artistic development.

○ Ask the singing teacher to come and deliver a one-off vocal workshop for the whole choir. Make sure to brief the teacher on the levels of proficiency you have in your choir and any particular area of weakness.

○ Involve your singing teacher when arranging solos or auditioning new singers and make sure you really make the most of their expertise.

○ Occasionally, ask the teacher to lead the warm-up. You might pick up some useful tips, and you can ensure that you are using the same terminology.

Bonus idea

The singing teacher could attend the final rehearsals in the lead-up to a concert. This could help to remind the singers of what they have worked on during their singing lessons, and how that feeds into the group sound.

A different pair of ears

"Our conductor tells us we're good, but I think she's just being nice!"

It can sometimes feel very lonely, leading each and every rehearsal, so why not bring in some guest conductors and experts to back up what you're saying?

Bonus idea

Don't view bringing other people in as a failure. It shows real humility, dedication and openness. Sometimes another pair of ears makes such a difference, and a slight alteration in the way an issue is addressed could be a real breakthrough moment.

O Underline some areas where your singers consistently struggle, and start to think about what kind of expert could make a difference or a positive change to your singers.

O Plan out a few sessions where you could work in conjunction with an external figure to make real headway in a project, perhaps nearer to a concert.

O Tell your choir that you're going to do this. Ask your singers what they're struggling with and where they would like additional input, and compile a 'triage list' for the visitor.

O Think big! Seek out some leading professionals and don't be scared to make direct contact. Many choral specialists get lots of requests for them to lead guest workshops and are more than happy to help if they can.

O If you're stuck for whom to ask, look at panellists and adjudicators from major choral competitions and festivals and see if you can get ideas from social media.

O It may not need to be a choral specialist – perhaps a movement director or percussionist's perspective would be useful.

Singing for each other

"I love the sound of my choir, but have no idea what we sound like individually!"

One of the best things to do as an alternative to working towards a performance is to simply enjoy each other's voices and musical tastes. Organise an occasion where everyone gets a chance to step into the limelight and be the soloist.

● Plan an informal recital of solos, duets and trios and ask all of your singers to take part.

● Give your singers lots of notice about this so that they have time to think about what they would like to contribute.

● You may find that some of your singers say, 'I joined a choir because I don't want to sing on my own'. But they may be open to preparing a duo or trio if given some gentle encouragement. The whole experience will be a positive step in developing the morale within your choir and will give everyone an insight into the array of voices that make up the ensemble.

● Allow people to sing music from any genre they want. You may find talents, voices and interests you didn't know you had, and perhaps the next Maria Callas!

● Schedule this event for a good time in the year when you're not too busy. It should not become an additional burden and add stress to your singers' lives.

● This could end up being a social closure to your season, complete with BBQ, Choir Awards, and a good old knees-up.

Top tip

Make a real effort to keep this a relaxed occasion with food and drink, and chairs and tables rather than a formal audience.

Sharing concerts

"Sometimes putting on a concert on my own is just too much. I wish I could team up with others."

One of the most enjoyable performance opportunities is when two or more choirs come together to share a concert. In doing this you halve the programme, halve the rehearsal burden, halve the organisation and, most importantly, double your audience!

Taking it further...

You could speak to a local sponsor or look into funding that supports collaborations and connections between different groups.

○ Check out local choirs and musical groups in your area.

○ Perhaps choose one that offers an interesting and audience-appealing contrast to the music of your choir.

○ Attend one of the other choir's concerts to show your support and then make contact with its musical director. Make sure you have already thought of some ideas of ways you could work together.

○ Consider two sets each (perhaps 15 minutes per set) and then discuss exciting collaborative ways to finish the concert in style altogether. Don't be afraid to suggest learning one of their pieces and vice versa – that's part of the fun.

○ Think about an interesting or eye-catching title that will let people know that this is a unique collaboration.

○ Share experiences and opinions on concert venues you have used.

○ Agree on who's going to pay for what and get this in writing so that there is no confusion later on.

○ Come together on promotion and make sure it is a combined effort.

○ Conduct the other choir and invite the other conductor to work with your group. This would not only mix things up a little but give each choir some new perspectives.

○ Choose your repertoire carefully. Make sure each group complements the other and that your programme is varied and interesting.

Get your wellies on!

"There are so many choir festivals in the UK, I just don't know where to begin."

Attend and perform at a big festival. It is an amazing and exciting experience for you and your singers, and could be a catalyst for so many other good things.

❍ Research choir festivals. Look at British Choirs on the Net, singacappella.org, the ABCD magazine, or *Choir & Organ* magazine's Choir Festival pull-out guide. And, of course, don't forget to look on forums and social media.

❍ Make a list of all of the festivals that might be appropriate for your choir, both home and abroad. Chorus! at London's Southbank Centre and the London A Cappella Festival are two big ones that you can look at in the UK, but there are many more.

❍ Most festivals welcome performances from visiting choirs. Start contacting organisers and see where your choir can join in.

❍ Be open minded about performing with others, or forming a larger group.

❍ If you're looking to perform a concert on your own, make yourselves sellable. Good photos, a decent website and recordings or videos you are proud of will go a long way, if you need to convince people that they should feature you in their line-up.

❍ If you are making the trip, let people know. Contact local press, post on social media, hand out flyers, sing about it in the streets, do everything! You never know who might be interested, or what it could lead to.

Top tip

If the festival involves substantial travel and overnight stays, schedule a concert, a special performance event or something nearby to make the most of the time.

Involving everyone

Not all of your singers need to be available to make a trip possible, so don't be afraid to go with a small number – but do involve everyone willing to make the trip.

Respecting the body

"Your choir sounds OK but you all look like a sack of potatoes!"

Everything about your singing is connected to your body. How you use it, understand it, and respect it will have a direct impact on how you sound.

○ Spend a special session focusing on respecting the body, posture and how to stand.

○ Remind your singers that knowing how to hold ourselves when we sing is as important as instrumentalists knowing how to hold their instrument – it's not an added extra. Our voice is our instrument, so hold it correctly.

○ Whether you are seated or standing, posture and alignment is crucial to allow your body to be free and to avoid possible obstruction of airflow.

○ Work with big mirrors so that your singers can see themselves and assess their own posture. It will make such a difference if they can see what they are doing and understand its importance.

○ Alexander Technique teachers work particularly to relieve the body from any unnecessary tension and re-educate it to make it more efficient. Could you get an Alexander Technique teacher to lead your session on the body or work with individuals who would benefit from some one-to-one attention?

○ Attend a local yoga or pilates class as a choir to reinforce the importance of posture and respecting your body.

A one off

"Sometimes I get an idea on the way home from rehearsals for something a little whacky to fix a problem and then it gets forgotten or put to one side. I wish I acted on it straight away."

Often you need to force yourself to act on ideas quickly. When you're reviewing a rehearsal and evaluating how things went and an idea comes to mind, take the plunge and plan something straight away.

○ After the rehearsal, ask yourself, 'What was that rehearsal missing?' or 'What didn't the singers understand?'

○ Speak to your section leaders and more senior singers, asking them for details of any causes for concern. They will feel empowered and develop more of a sense of duty to work through things if you involve them.

○ Decide what type of approach the singers would benefit from. Do they need to focus on a technical aspect and spend more time on it, or do they need a different approach, perhaps led by someone from outside of the choir?

○ Be bold and make this a reality. Schedule some time for this as soon as possible.

○ Re-work the rest of your schedule to accommodate this. Don't worry too much about its impact on other rehearsals – fixing the problem will make a huge difference to the overall workings of the choir.

○ Whether it is a musicianship element or one of vocal technique, addressing it can transform the rest of your rehearsals and performances.

Taking it further...

There are many experts, choral consultants and vocal tutors who would relish the chance to come and work in such a focused and detailed way. Many of the top choirs throughout the world are changing their perceptions about external help and it's creating quite a buzz, so why not join in?

Part 8
Surviving in leadership

It's not about you

"I used to have a horrendous choir master. I never want to be like that."

Starting a choir for selfless reasons isn't possible all the time. You want the choir to be great, entertaining, worthwhile, fun, powerful and successful, and all of these reflect on you. Sometimes we have to deal with our own issues first before we start running a choir.

Taking it further...

Have a network of people outside of choir who can support you and who you can ask for advice. Choose people who will challenge you and tell you honestly if you are approaching things in the wrong way.

Leadership of choirs is a very rewarding, challenging and responsible task. You are working with people who will feel vulnerable, inadequate, proud, arrogant, scared, nervous and victorious in the journey you take together.

It is important that you are clear and critical of your motivation for leadership of a choir. Keep these motives constructive and beneficial to your singers and audiences – it's not all about you, and you want to give people an opportunity to have a great choir experience making wonderful music. That choir experience comes from you as the leader, and the person that you are will shape the way you lead the group.

It can be easy to want to be in control of everything, to want the choir and its decisions to be 'yours' and to be hesitant about delegation and giving singers opportunities they need if these won't create 'perfect' results. If you have tendencies to keep too much control, slowly break these and learn to let others control areas, to delegate and to ask for input and opinions from others. Hold the choir loosely – it's a joint ownership, and only succeeds with a group effort. Share in the failures, and share the glory.

Friend vs Leader

"I'm good friends with some of the singers in my choirs. Is this a good thing?"

The relationship that you have with your members will have a direct impact on their motivation and development. Working so closely with so many people, you will inevitably draw close attachments to your singers but you must learn to strike a balance between friend and leader. Being friendly with all of your singers is great but becoming too close to certain members may cause frictions.

● Your choir should be thought of as a professional environment and should be treated as such.

● There must be some clear boundaries so that the levels of leadership are maintained. Even when socialising, it is best to maintain the same boundaries.

● Always be friendly, but if you get too close your singers will start to see a clique forming around you. They may resent those people who are becoming closer to you.

● You may find yourself giving more of your time and more exciting opportunities to your friends because you feel that they are dependable and trustworthy.

● You cannot appear to favour any individual members above anyone else. Show any favouritism and you will soon start to lose respect.

● Your singers need to know that they can come to you with a private issue secure in the knowledge that you will not discuss it with anyone else. If you have a circle of friends who you seem to discuss all things with, you will be creating a potential lack of trust.

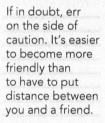

Top tip

If in doubt, err on the side of caution. It's easier to become more friendly than to have to put distance between you and a friend.

Getting respect as a leader

"How do I get respect from my choir members?"

You want your choir members to respect you as their musical leader, but this won't be automatic. Work hard at being the best you can be, at making time for the group, and they will appreciate all you do.

Top tip

Never expect perfection either from yourself or from your choir. It's not possible, and if that's what you're after you will never be satisfied.

❍ Plan and be confident in what you're doing. Always make sure you know the songs inside out and try to predict what your choir might struggle with. That way you can prepare some exercises to help tackle that challenge, or you can think about the best way to explain how to correct any errors in that area.

❍ Be organised. Make sure you always have a schedule and a plan so that you never forget to arrange something for a concert and you never miss out on any exciting events.

❍ Be consistent. Always maintain a professional approach in every rehearsal.

❍ Be punctual. Make sure you are getting to the concerts on time too, and lead by example.

❍ Be responsive. Answer telephone calls and emails promptly and deal with choir issues both personal and professional as quickly as possible.

❍ Be transparent. State clearly what you want to achieve and what you expect from the choir.

❍ Be comfortable admitting when you're wrong. You will make mistakes at times.

❍ Forgive mistakes and move on.

❍ Support those that need it.

❍ Be courageous. Make sure that every now and again you take a risk, take yourself out of your comfort zone or try something new.

I can't sing!

"I'm not a singer. Can I still lead a choir?"

Many choir leaders are not singers and it's not a prerequisite to directing a choir. The skills required to be an excellent singer are vastly different from the skills required to be an excellent teacher or director. An orchestral conductor would never be expected to play every instrument, and similarly, you don't need to be a singer. If you have a good knowledge of music there's no reason you can't direct a choir.

○ Learn about the voice as an instrument and what is required as a singer. Research singing technique and understand the difficulties that singers face.

○ Be honest about your ability and where your strengths lie. Never try to make out that you are better than you are, as your choir will quickly see through this.

○ Develop your voice and get some training from a professional voice coach. This is not to turn you into a singer but so that you can see the process involved in improving and working on your voice, and understand what aspects of singing are difficult.

○ Describe your warm-ups and exercises in speech rather than demonstrating, and find resources that do vocal demonstrations for you.

○ Demonstrate phrases of sections that need improving on your instrument (whatever that might be). Many directors play keyboard instruments, which helps, as they have the full pitch range of a choir at their fingertips and can play accompaniments.

○ Work with an accompanist who can demonstrate phrases on the piano or keyboard. Singers should learn to be able to reproduce what they hear from any instrument or voice, so this is a useful skill for them to learn.

Involving everyone

If you feel that a vocal demonstration would be particularly useful, why not ask one of the singers that you know understands the passage to demonstrate? It will give them a confidence boost.

First steps as a conductor

"I inherited this position as there wasn't anyone else willing to at the time, but I'm not sure I'm any good."

If taking the helm and conducting a choir is new to you, relax and follow these steps. It doesn't have to be daunting or stressful.

Top tip

Get to know the voices in your choir and hold some voice assessments. Develop a member profile with details, range information, vocal strengths and targets for the future.

Bonus idea

If you are joining an existing choir, trying to make radical changes too quickly is a bad idea. In your first few terms, you should respect their traditions and focus on doing a great job.

❍ Think about your targets and why you're there. Who inspired you to do this? What did they do to inspire you? What do you want to try and do to improve this choir? How can you make a difference? Note these down and keep them for reference.

❍ Don't let repertoire or technically challenging pieces scare you. There is no pressure to do anything too tricky, so start simply and set yourself achievable goals.

❍ Don't apologise for your gestures and style – any conductor takes time to establish a style and character.

❍ Don't be afraid to make mistakes. Give the task your all and learn from the mistakes you will inevitably make.

❍ Ask other conductors of nearby choirs if you can watch them work. Take note of what makes it easy for the singers to follow the conductor and what techniques you could adopt.

❍ If you have to pick up projects already planned, make sure you know exactly what is expected and devise a rehearsal schedule. If it feels overwhelming, think of ways to simplify things.

❍ Film yourself and assess what you like and dislike about your style and how you come across to singers.

Don't stop, never give up

"The day I stop learning is the day I should stop leading."

As a conductor and leader, you must remember that you don't have all the answers, and as with any other job, you should always be challenging yourself to improve, both for the sake of the choir and for your own job satisfaction.

○ Look ahead at the coming year and schedule two or three times to attend development sessions (CPD) or workshops.

○ One of these sessions could coincide with the start of a new term, so you arrive back with new ideas and approaches fresh in your mind.

○ Get in touch with your local Music Hub to find out about its CPD sessions, particularly any specially aimed at vocal leaders. If the Music Hub does not provide one, see if you can convince it to add one to the programme.

○ Join an organisation which supports music makers and runs training events. (Explore Making Music, Association of British Choral Directors, London A Cappella Festival or Voice Festival UK.)

○ Consider attending a conducting course. These are available at a variety of levels, so you should be able to find something suitable for you.

○ Find conductors to shadow – they could be orchestral or wind band conductors as well as choral leaders. Most professional conductors will allow you to watch a session, so be bold and get in touch.

Top tip

Be honest with yourself. List your shortcomings and areas where you could improve.

Bonus idea

Get together with other leaders and conductors who are interested in developing their skills and go to an event as a group. Better still, create your own event, watch each other conduct and debrief together in a social atmosphere afterwards.

Shared responsibility

"I don't think I ever come back from rehearsals or concerts in a state other than utterly exhausted. I don't feel I get a chance to enjoy leading and standing in front of my choir and appreciating all our hard work."

You are in charge of your choir. You're there to instruct, encourage, correct, organise and support your singers, but that doesn't mean that the effort and responsibility solely rests with you.

○ It is essential to delegate and allow your choir to take responsibility for various aspects of performance, administration and development. Administration, finances and logistical planning can all be delegated. It's a healthy choir when members are meeting and discussing things without you.

○ There may come a time when you are not the leader any more, or when you are absent for some reason and your choir needs to be able to continue.

○ You will inevitably be absent for a rehearsal, so appoint an assistant conductor to work with you, learn the repertoire and be ready to stand in if needed. Perhaps that person should then be given the chance to conduct some pieces in performance. The benefits for the choir and you are endless: you'll get to hear them, assess and experience a different side to them and you will know that things can happen without you.

○ Positive attitudes towards working with other conductors are life-giving for a choir – and a sign of versatility and inner-confidence. The more the singers get used to working and responding to other leaders, the better they will be. You might get asked to be part of a big project where your choir is hired and you are just there to rehearse and handover, which can open up some great experiences for the group.

DIY: Do it yourself

"I'm nervous about singing in front of my choir but I know that they would benefit from demonstrations instead of me explaining every time."

When it comes to singing, it can often be hard to explain what you mean with words, and the easiest way to explain something is to show your choir how to do it. Develop your confidence in this area.

○ Singing in front of any group of people can be daunting, but be confident and you will sound convincing.

○ Make sure to know the music inside out before teaching it, then if you do need to demonstrate something you'll be well prepared.

○ When demonstrating, don't sing just the right notes but also the correct dynamics, shape of the phrase, posture and diction. You don't want to correct one element to discover that singers have copied an error in a different area that you made.

○ If you make a mistake, don't worry, just start again. Either tell the singers what you did wrong (so they know not to copy it) or ask them what you did wrong.

○ When you are demonstrating an idea, your singers should not look to emulate your voice. Your demonstration is a way to convey an idea, but you want them to sing it with their voices. Ask them to repeat it back to you to check they have understood what you were trying to convey.

○ You may find that some of your singers struggle with interpreting your demonstration, especially if they have a different voice type. Be patient while they get used to how your voice sounds and work out how to translate your demonstration to their own vocal instrument.

Involving everyone

Often a direction is for everyone, so get everyone to listen and respond collectively. Choose a phrase and ask all singers to sing it together in the required way, regardless of whether it's their part or not.

Idea 85

Metaphors and imagery

"Sometimes I find it so difficult to explain what I mean when instructing my singers. Words and markings don't always do it for me."

One of the most difficult things about instructing singers is that you can't see or hold your instrument, so sometimes trying to explain things to singers can be quite tricky. Metaphors and imagery are often a great way to go about explaining things.

Prepare in advance. Listen to recordings of the music and try and visualise images or metaphors that might convey the mood of the song.

Sing it through and consider the more challenging parts of the song. Think about what you do physically to get the right sound. Again, try and think of images or metaphors associated with what you're doing. For example:

Involving everyone

Explain how you want a phrase to sound and ask singers who are achieving this to explain their approach.

○ If you have a particularly high note, instruct your singers to imagine that you are lifting yourself above the note and looking down on it.

○ If you need your choir to project, tell the singers that there is an elderly audience member with hearing issues and they need to project loud enough for her to hear.

○ For posture, tell them to imagine that they have a piece of string attached to the top of their head and they are dangling from it.

When introducing imagery, make sure everyone understands, and get people to write the metaphor or imagery into their scores, if they are finding it useful.

All your singers can be involved in visualising their sound and their vocal delivery. Ask them with their eyes closed to experiment with some physical gestures related to the music they're singing.

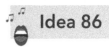

Singing lingo

"Sometimes I get the feeling that what I say to the choir isn't going in or making sense. Am I explaining it well enough?"

When you have so many singers with diverse musical backgrounds, it's often easier just to use simple terminology or use words which mean something to everyone.

● It is possible that some members of your choir will not have extensive knowledge of Italian musical terms and others will have little experience of annotating a musical score. Be careful that everyone understands every instruction and notes something which will help them remember it accurately. Ask individuals to explain it back to the rest of the group.

● 'Diminuendo', 'anacrusis', 'fermata' are all words that work equally well in English, so use 'getting quieter', 'an upbeat'' and 'pause'. Don't be embarrassed to be simple and straightforward – there is no point using words you find useful if your singers do not.

● When talking about technique, avoid overly scientific terminology and try and use words that help the process seem simpler to achieve.

● Use a conducting gesture as you give your instruction. This way you're showing what you want as well as telling the choir.

● Ask your singers how they would best describe particular techniques you have taught, and listen to the vocabulary they use to explain them. Sharing these with other singers may be beneficial and resonate with some individuals.

Bonus idea

Create a phrasebook of musical expressions and terminology to give to your singers. Follow this by explaining exactly what each and every word means, and how you put it into practice.

🎤 Part 9
Making your voice heard

Make some noise

"I don't know where to start."

If you're trying to get people to your concert, there are lots of things you can do. Here's a whistlestop tour through a few of them, but be careful to target people who are near enough to travel to hear you.

Taking it further...

Look into mailing websites (like mailchimp.com) which allow you to send professional looking emails to large mailing lists, allows people to subscribe and unsubscribe and keeps your lists up to date.

● BBC Radio 3's *The Choir* has a feature called 'Meet My Choir'. Get in touch to see if your group could be featured.

● Local, university and hospital radio. Would a local radio station like your group to visit their studio and tell them about your next concert and, better still, sing a short piece? Make a phone call and find out.

● Blogs, vlogs and podcasts. Edit together a sample of your rehearsals and interviews with singers to convey what makes your project worth hearing and supporting.

● Local area newsletters. If the community around your venue has a newsletter or well-read magazine, this may be the perfect place for some coverage of your story.

● Busking and flashmobs. Give people a taste of your music in a busy community space.

● Listings! Make sure you're in local guides and e-newsletters and, for national press, contact the Press Association.

● Build a mailing list. Ask people for their email addresses at concerts so that you can keep in touch and create an audience of regulars.

Concert titles

"I'm not going to that, it sounds boring."

Getting the concert title right is very important when you're trying to attract an audience and create media interest, so think about it carefully. These are some tips to bear in mind.

❍ Examine your programme and consider the core theme and reasons behind choosing the repertoire.

❍ With the theme and reasons for your repertoire choices in mind, mindmap a list of words they inspire (you can do this with the choir too).

❍ Be imaginative but don't pick something so unusual that people won't understand.

❍ Pick a title that's modern, meaningful and relates to the type of audience you're trying to attract.

❍ Puns and jokes are always fun.

❍ Keep it clear and comprehensible for the general public.

❍ If there is a particularly popular piece in the programme, consider using this as a concert name.

❍ Your title should convey what your audience can expect from the concert.

❍ Make your title short and punchy. Long and wordy titles take away the impact.

❍ Do some research and take inspiration from existing concert titles.

❍ Be decisive. Not everyone in the choir will agree, so make the final call.

❍ Integrate your title with social media campaigns, for example incorporating a hashtag.

❍ Within the title, consider including reference to whether your concert is specific to a certain time of year.

Bonus idea

Look at CDs that have songs from your programme on them and take inspiration from the album titles. Record companies know how to be commercial.

Read all about it!

"Our flyers always look a bit dated and messy. How do I create something a bit more professional looking without spending loads of money?"

An eye-catching, well designed flyer is a great way to spread the word about your next concert and grab people's attention. Just make sure they get well distributed.

Bonus idea

Ask the venue about advertising your concert at other events in the lead-up to yours. See if someone would be willing to hand out flyers to those audiences and whether you could insert them into programmes at other concerts, or leave some by the entrance or bar.

O Do some research – go to prominent concert venues and look at their flyers. Collate the ones you like, and work out what is attracting you. Make a list of the features and aspects that catch your eye.

O Make sure your design is eye-catching and conveys what you are – a great choir!

O Have a house style for your flyers so that all of your promotional materials look similar. It creates consistency and familiarity so people recognise your materials from a distance. Pick a good font that is easy to read.

O Be careful about using photos of the singers – these date very quickly and may not convey the music you are performing.

O Focus on the theme of the concert and do a mindmap of images this conjures up. One may make a great eye-catching design.

O Give all information necessary, but keep it to the minimum. Include the concert title, choir name, a short description of event, venue, date and time, website and how to buy tickets.

O Think about the size of flyers. If they are to share with friends they need to be small and easy to put in a bag or inside a diary.

Social media savvy

"We've got a Facebook page but we have very few likes. How do I get people engaged?"

Twitter, Facebook and Instagram each have millions of worldwide users – it really couldn't be easier to get your choir seen, but it can also be easy to get lost.

○ Have a username or handle that is the same across all platforms. If you go by one name on Twitter, something else on Facebook, and so on, you will make it harder for people to find you.

○ Similarly, have one image across your social media and try to use high-quality images.

○ Connect all of your accounts so that when you post something in one place, it posts to them all. This means that your fans or members see everything, regardless of which platform they use.

○ Follow people that you think would be interested in you: other choirs, singing teachers, choir fans, friends of your choir members and local businesses. Once people know you are there they will be able to engage with you and your following will start to grow. Don't wait for people to find you.

Bonus idea

Consider paying for promoted tweets and posts. It's relatively inexpensive and is a quick way of getting more visibility. Test the water by spending a small amount of money and measure its success before spending any more.

○ Post regularly. Even if you don't feel you have anything new to say, there's always something you can share. If users visit your profile and see you don't use it regularly they are unlikely to revisit your page.

○ Engage with your followers. Reply to comments, ask questions, involve people through online ticket competitions. The more you engage, the more followers you'll accumulate.

○ Have fun with it! Continuously try new things: fun videos, pictures, hashtags, and so on. Some things will work and some things may not, but keep trying and you'll start to find the things your followers engage with the most.

We are family: your choral community

"I want to get involved in more choral music events and meet other choirs. How do I do this?"

If you've got enthusiastic singers who want to make more music, keep looking outwards to see what else you can get involved in.

Taking it further...

Handy URLs: British Choirs on the Net (www.choirs.org.uk), Making Music (makingmusic.org.uk), ABCD (abcd.org.uk), London A Cappella Festival (londonacappella festival.com)

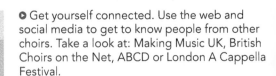

Bonus idea

Create a festival or big event of your own and invite other choirs within your area for an epic performance!

❍ Get yourself connected. Use the web and social media to get to know people from other choirs. Take a look at: Making Music UK, British Choirs on the Net, ABCD or London A Cappella Festival.

❍ Join forums, discussions and online chats to find out what is going on and follow leading conductors, choirs and choral festivals on social media to stay updated with what they are doing. Look at all genres and be open minded.

❍ BBC Radio 3 has some great programmes of choral music including *The Choir*. Listen in, and where there are opportunities for choirs to be featured, get involved!

❍ You will be surrounded by schools, colleges and universities wherever you are, so why not get in touch and connect with their groups? Even if your choir demographic does not match theirs they may well have events which are open. Push doors and see which open and where they lead. Making contact with other choirs can only be fruitful in the long term, even if you don't see it immediately.

❍ Invite people from the wider musical network to your concerts, offering free tickets. See if they may be willing to speak to your choir about what they do.

Who needs a website?

"Do I really need a website to run a choir?"

A lot of people believe that anything they would have on a website would be better served by Facebook and Twitter, but there is so much more you can do with a website. With a website, you will be able to sell tickets and merchandise directly from your site, have an events calendar – and it looks professional. But where do you start?

○ Get all your materials together: pictures from the latest concert, rehearsal shots, videos, blogs, links to your social media pages, audio samples, general information and contact information. All of this will make for a very strong website and a place where the general public can find you and contact you.

○ Choose a domain name. Use your choir name or your social media username. If these are already taken, then think outside the box, but make sure the name conveys what you are.

○ Build your website. There are many free website creators such as Weebly, Moonfruit, Sitebuilder and Sitey. Choose a house style and stick to it.

○ Do a thorough proofread before you launch your site. Check words are spelled correctly, that all links and videos work and that your contact details and information are correct. Then ask a couple of other people to look at it with fresh eyes.

○ When you've built your site and are ready to launch it, advertise it everywhere. Put it on all promotional material and social media, and spread news of its existence through word of mouth.

Involving everyone

If you are feeling in the party mood, have a website launch party. It's a great excuse for an informal concert. Be sure to invite anyone who helped you create the site, friends and family, and those who support your choir in other ways (for example accompanists and contacts from your rehearsal venue).

Great news travels fast

"I've emailed and tweeted and texted and WhatsApped, but no one wants to come to the concert."

Word of mouth is the original social media and word travels fast! Before Twittter, Facebook, emails and Instagrams were thought of, we put our ideas out there using our voices. There is still power in the word of mouth.

Taking it further...

If you are not the talking type, perhaps you could ask someone to deliver the message for you. Could you get some choir 'ambassadors' from the choir or outside to capture your vision, talk about it, and network on your behalf?

❍ Talk about your choir in normal conversation. Whether you want to get a new choir off the ground or inject some new life and opportunities into your existing choir, you need to talk about the choir like it is the best thing ever in the world. Talk about it with whoever will listen.

❍ Tell people your plans for the future. What gigs do you have coming up, who have you booked in for a workshop later in the year, what will you be doing this year that you didn't do last year, and how has the choir evolved recently? If you get excited about the choir, other people will.

❍ Ask your singers to do the same – 30 voices are louder than one.

❍ When you speak to people encourage them to spread the word and to tell someone they think may be interested in joining the choir or coming to a concert.

❍ Invite people personally to concerts. An email can feel impersonal, but if you give people a telephone call and ask them to join you they will see that it is important to you that they are there.

❍ Ask your singers to invite people personally, using their voices. The power of an individual conversation and the time that takes will make people want to respond to you positively.

Part 10
Technology

Idea 94

Make a video

"One of the reasons I chose this choir is because someone sent me a link to a video they'd made."

We live in a fast-paced world, with huge amounts of information at our fingertips. The way you connect needs to be fast paced and instantly accessible too – enable people to see you sing at the very moment they want to!

Taking it further...

If you want a very slick sound recording, consider recording the audio first and then miming to its playback for your video.

Bonus idea ★

If you don't have anyone who is handy with cameras and editing, get in touch with a local university or college to see if a film/media student could help out.

○ Choose one of the pieces you have worked on as a suitable item to be filmed in a special promotional video. Make sure you know it well and ideally can perform it off by heart.

○ Consider whether you want a straight recording of a piece, or if you have video editing capabilities, a 'docu-video' – a video with interviews from members and shots of the choir in rehearsal, giving a snapshot of who you are personally as well as musically.

○ Get in touch with someone with a camera, or find a digital camera which records videos. It doesn't need to be Hollywood, just clear.

○ If you have someone with video editing capabilities, consider filming from more than one static camera, or having both static and moving shots.

○ Pick a suitable venue to film in, somewhere where the lighting can be manipulated and the backdrop will catch the eye.

○ Decide the style and ambience you are aiming for, and tie together everything visual: lighting, what aspects of the venue are in view, and what the singers wear.

○ Press record and perform to your very best! Engage your audience, even though you cannot see them.

Up in the cloud

"We would love to get our music out there but we have no idea where to start and we have no money."

Share your music. It will give your choir a boost and it doesn't need to be expensive or top quality.

Since its launch in 2007, SoundCloud has become a leading online platform for people to share sounds. You don't need a record contract or money, and it's easy to use. It has millions of users, so if you want lots of people to hear your music, this is a great place.

Create an account for free and upload an mp3 recording from your computer. You can even make live recordings on your phone and upload them directly to the site using the SoundCloud app. Once your choir's music is up there, it will be available for anyone to listen to for free and there is also an option to make your song free to download. Listeners can also 'like', 'share' and add comments to each track, so you have the opportunity to get some useful feedback. Embed your SoundCloud tracks on your website, so people can read about you, see pictures of you and hear you all in one place.

Taking it further...

This should encourage you to bite the bullet and record your choir – see Idea 67 for how to do this well just using smartphones. If you are lucky enough to have the money, book a session in a recording studio.

Bonus idea

If you could sell CDs to friends and family, could you ring-fence this income to put towards future recordings?

Creating a professional recording

"I want to make a professional recording of my choir to sell. Where do I start?"

If your choir has been running for a while, you have a good repertoire of songs behind you and have a decent-sized fan base,
then you should definitely look at creating a professional recording.

Taking it further...

Think about the artwork of your disc – what could you use as the front cover of your album? Write a biography about your choir to be included on the jacket and try and source a few good reviews or quotes from audience members to include.

○ Decide what you want to record. Are you recording a covers album? An EP of original material? A single? Whatever it is, make sure that your singers know the songs like the back of their hand. Recording studios are expensive and you can't afford to be learning parts or fixing mistakes in the studio.

○ Carefully order your tracklist as you would for a concert programme. If this includes copyright works you will need to register the disc with the collecting societies (MCPS at prsformusic.com) to ensure that you have the correct licences.

○ Choose a suitable professional studio that will accommodate your choir. Smaller choirs will find it easier to find spaces. Large choirs may have to divide themselves and record in smaller groups. Remember, studios are not cheap, so do a lot of research. You will be charged on time, so while a smaller place may be cheaper, if it will take longer this will be a false economy.

○ If you need musicians on the recording, book them into the studio for an earlier session. While a rough backing to the tracks is all that is needed to record the choir, it is better to have something as close to the finished sound as possible to get the true feel.

○ Source someone to mix and master the disc.

○ You will need a CD duplicator to create the number of CDs that you require. Be realistic with how many you think you'll be able to sell. Take into account the number of singers in your choir, their families, your fans and any freebies you might want to give away.

○ You will need an online music aggregator to get your music onto iTunes, Spotify, Amazon and other online music retailers. They charge fees, so do some research on what would be best for you. Good examples include CD Baby (cdbaby.com) and TuneCore (tunecore.co.uk).

○ Work out what you need to pay to get the recording to market and stick to that budget.

○ Consider the total amount that you have spent on creating your recording, marketing and any other costs and come up with a realistic selling price.

○ Sell, sell, sell, and don't forget to take them to all your gigs!

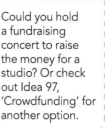

Bonus idea

Could you hold a fundraising concert to raise the money for a studio? Or check out Idea 97, 'Crowdfunding' for another option.

Idea 97

Crowdfunding

"I need to record my choir but we have no money. Help!"

Crowdfunding is a great way to fund a project. The way it works is that you ask fans to donate and in return you give them something by way of thanks. Your supporters help you out, and get something in return.

Taking it further...

Crowdfunding websites are a great way to share the story and administer the campaign, but if you have people willing to help, there is no reason why you couldn't do this all yourself.

Top tip

Bear in mind that the crowdfunding platform will charge a percentage (often about 15%) on the money raised, and some only give money if your target is achieved. Read the small print.

❍ Choose any one of the many crowdfunding sites. (Pledgemusic.com, Kickstarter.com and Crowdfunder.co.uk are good places to start for a music project.)

❍ Begin your campaign. Write a concise biography about your choir and state clearly what you want to achieve. Do you want to make an EP? Are you trying to get funding to do a tour? Explain why you need your supporters' help and why you can't fund it yourself.

❍ Work out what finance you need for your project. Be realistic and take into account costs like studio time, mixing, mastering, duplication, artwork and distribution, plus any fees for musicians accompanying your choir.

❍ Explain what you will give in return for the financial support. For example, you may give a public 'thank you' on Twitter for a £5 donation, a signed CD for £15 donations, allow people to be present at a recording session and to get a free CD for a larger sum. Be creative! Get inspiration from other successful campaigns.

❍ Launch your campaign and tell everyone about it. Tweet about it, mention it at gigs, talk about it, put it on your website and across all your social media. The quicker you spread the news, the quicker your project will be funded.

Making your CD legally

"We've recorded an album and want to start selling it. Do we need a licence for that?"

If you are recording other people's music, you need to make sure you do this properly so that the songwriters are properly remunerated.

Recording an album of favourite songs and pieces is an easy way for most choirs to showcase their music. Songs that people know and love may be easier to sell at gigs and other events, but this does mean that you should get a licence to take care of all royalty payments back to the writer where required, and a MCPS-PPL Limited Manufacture Licence will probably suit your needs. This is suitable for scenarios where you are selling directly to fans and friends, and creating fewer than 1,000 copies. If you are selling more and through retailers or distributors, you will need to look into the AP licences. Visit prsformusic.com for full information. If you have re-arranged the original work and it is no longer a cover, you need to seek permission from the copyright holder in addition to getting the correct licence.

If you sign up with an online music aggregator to make your tracks available for download, the licensing will be looked after on your behalf. Using an online music aggregator will spread your music far and wide and their licences cover worldwide use, but be sure to check the small print.

Taking it further...

If you have created a recording that is completely your own music you don't need any licences, but you may want to register as a songwriter with the PRS yourself and add the songs to your works list.

Mashing and looping

"There are some new kids on the block chatting about going loopy with mashed potato – what are they talking about?"

Mashing and looping are becoming very much part of the choral and vocal world and are probably here to stay, so give them a go and see what sounds are produced!

Taking it further...

Helpful URLs!
The Swingles
(theswingles.co.uk),
The Real Group
(therealgroup.se),
Katy Tunstall
(kttunstall.com),
Jamie Woon
(jamiewoon.com),
Shlomo
(shlomobeatbox.
co.uk), Beardyman
(beardyman.co.uk),
Pentatonix
(ptxofficial.com),
Greg Beardsell's
'Making Mash'
video (prezi.com/
qsbb2pgq_zrr/
making-mash).

◗ Looping and mashing are two ways to create accessible, easy, inclusive and infectious new sounds and devise new pieces, so don't hesitate to get involved.

◗ Live looping is the electronic recording and playback of a vocal fragment or riff, which your choir can then sing over, adding layers. You can also layer recorded loops on top of each other to build texture and provide a bigger vocal accompaniment than your number of singers may otherwise allow.

◗ The Swingles, The Real Group, Ed Sheeran, Katy Tunstall and Jamie Woon, all have great examples of using looping and these should inspire you. Once you've done some research and have some ideas of ways to start, see if you can borrow a looping pedal and equipment and experiment. Start simple, perhaps with a round, so you can get a feel for how it works and what may sound good for your ensemble.

◗ Looping can also be simulated without technology, by means of repeating segments of pieces in your voice parts or sections. Perhaps some voices move on to new melodies while some continue to repeat a short fragment.

● Mashing is when layers of different songs (of any genre) are combined. Check out the wonderful Shlomo, Beardyman, and Pentatonix for beatbox and mash medley ideas.

● Mashing and looping do have rules. The riffs and segments must fit together harmonically.

● The most successful and super-catchy examples often involve music in the minor key. These have more emphasis on sevenths and fifths within the key structure, and sound really strong and weighty.

● Experiment and learn as much from what doesn't work as from what does. Record clips and play them back on top of each other, or meet with a friend to layer things acoustically and see what combines well.

Bonus idea

For a great example of how to mash, have a look at Greg Beardsell's 'Making Mash' on prezi.com, which gives you step-by-step instructions.

Making technology work for you

"My singers are always plugged into their devices. Should I embrace the technology or unplug?"

The simple answer is that we can't really get away from technology, so we should embrace it with both hands and feet – it's here to stay!

Involving everyone

Cater for *your* singers. Trying to use gadgets just for the sake of it is a waste of time if your singers don't find them useful.

Anecdote

Use supporting resources in the early stages of rehearsing and then be set free. Singers reading from tablets on stage is not how my choir dream ends, and is no better than being glued to paper lyric sheets or scores!

Mark

Whether you teach from scores or by ear, gadgets, apps or websites that can help with the learning of both words and music are really useful. Here are some ways you can make your life easier by being connected.

● Use a shared folder (e.g. Google Drive or Dropbox) that your singers can instantly access.

● Share markings, notes and annotations of your sheet music or lyrics and ask singers to write them into their own copies in advance of a rehearsal.

● Pronunciation guides – if you are singing in a tricky language, consider making 'crib sheets' available for singers between rehearsals.

● Spotify / iTunes links – point singers towards excellent recordings to inspire and get a sense of the music before you begin practising.

● Collaborative documents and calendars – if your singers can see and edit documents and calendars they can access up-to-date information so you don't need to circulate new copies and endless emails.

● There are websites and apps with useful music gadgets, like warm-ups, metronomes and pitch pipes so singers can find their notes at home even if they don't have an instrument.